Frigid Embrace

Politics, Economics, and Environment in Alaska

**Other titles in the
Culture and Environment in the Pacific West Series**

Series Editor: William L. Lang

Frigid Embrace

Politics, Economics, and Environment in Alaska

❧ ❧

Stephen Haycox

Oregon State University Press
Corvallis

For Dagmar,
with enduring gratitude

⚭

The paper in this book meets the guidelines for permanence and durability
of the Committee on Production Guidelines for Book Longevity of the
Council on Library Resources and the minimum requirements of the
American National Standard for Permanence of Paper for Printed Library
Materials Z39.48-1984.

Library of Congress Cataloging-in-Publication Data
Haycox, Stephen W.
  Politics, economics, and the environment in Alaska / by Stephen
Haycox.— 1st ed.
      p. cm. — (Culture and environment in the Pacific West)
Includes index.
  ISBN 0-87071-536-4 (alk. paper)
  1. Alaska—Civilization. 2. Alaska—Environmental conditions. 3.
Alaska—Economic conditions. 4. Human ecology—Alaska—History. 5.
Nature—Effect of human beings on—Alaska. 6. Frontier and pioneer
life—Alaska. 7. Pioneers—Alaska—Attitudes—History. 8. Indians of
North America—Alaska—History. I. Title. II. Series.
  F904 .H26 2002
  979.8—dc21

                                        2001005633

Oregon State University Press
101 Waldo Hall
Corvallis OR 97331-6407
541-737-3166 • fax 541-737-3170
http://oregonstate.edu/dept/press

OREGON STATE
UNIVERSITY

Series Editor's Preface

Alaska may be the epitome of the myth of American exceptionalism. It is at once an extreme representation of the idea that America is beyond comparison, and literally an exceptional place of natural and cultural extremes. Alaskan tourist promotions trumpet the idea, and the state has a long and powerful history that appears to justify the image. From the time William Henry Seward pushed through its purchase from Russia in 1867, Alaska has offered residents of the "lower 48" a destination and a reference point for wilderness, frontier, and isolation. In ways entrancing and surprising, the idea of Alaska has combined elements of an extreme environment and a spartan culture. Alaska was America's last landed frontier, a kind of hyperbolic extension of all the nation's previous frontiers, even as it replicated similar enthusiasms about earlier boomer destinations. It was a place of rushes and excitements: pelagic furs in the eighteenth and nineteenth centuries; gold in the early twentieth; fish, timber, and finally oil in the late twentieth. In each episode, Alaska has been portrayed as a cultural extremity, a place far removed but rich for the daring and resourceful.

From the beginning, culture and the environment combined to create a myth about Alaska that hyped the larger American myth. There is no denying the powerful pull Alaska's exotic image had on the immigrants to that far-north land. But how the new settlers understood their relationships with the monumental Alaskan environment and how they created their lives are different questions. In *Frigid Embrace*, Stephen Haycox focuses on how Alaskan settlers lived out their dreams. He calls his book a "historical commentary," because it is only through the lens of history that we can understand the larger pattern of relationships between environment and culture that dominate Alaskan society. Haycox asks a central question: how have Alaskan settlers' ideas about their environment affected and directed their approaches to indigenous people and the region's natural resource wealth? The answer is complex. As Haycox points out, migrants to Alaska have embraced the idea of wilderness, but they have resisted becoming wilderness residents. Alaskans saw nature as economic opportunity and they have defended their perceived right to open, unfettered access to ores, fisheries, forests, furs, and more, even if the chief agents of development lived far removed from Alaska.

Haycox argues that Alaskans have a colonial mindset that puts them at the mercy of both outside political and economic forces, while they often act themselves like transients. The result is a culture that exploits its nature, while it rhetorically embraces the beatitudes of wilderness. It is, as Haycox explains, an oppositional culture, one that looks at society as a set of binary relationships: Native and non-Native; environmentalist and developer; insider and outsider.

Alaskans are not the only westerners to exhibit these tendencies. Earlier boomer societies have perceived themselves and the world in similar ways, but Alaska is distinct because of its size and importance to the nation. It contains most of the nation's designated wilderness, the greatest expanse of roadless areas, the largest national forest, the most extensive region of snow, mountains, and ice, the largest known oil reserves, and a physical isolation that ranks second only to Hawaii. Alaska is what the tourist brochures proclaim: a place of wilderness dreams and experiences. America projects its historic conflict with wilderness on Alaska, leaving the resolution in Alaska's hands.

What Haycox has described and explained is the nation's last effort at denying its heritage of using and abusing the environment in the name of culture. It is a sobering story. *Frigid Embrace* documents and comments on one of the quintessential encounters between culture and environment in the American West. The myth of the West, Haycox concludes, prospers in Alaska perhaps as in no other place. This book reminds us that how people understand their environment—what values they place on nature—and how they imagine living in their environment—what values they place on community—defines much more than settling up a frontier area and building an economy. How we work out the relationships between culture and environment determines a dominant percentage of our lives in the Pacific West.

William L. Lang

Contents

꒦ ꒦

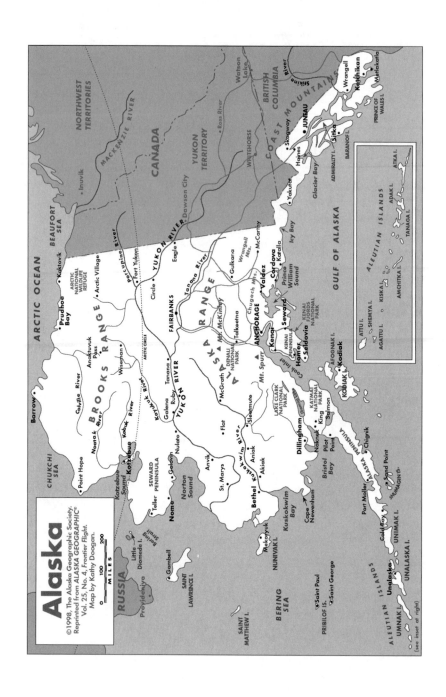

Map of Alaska. (Courtesy Alaska Geographic Society)

Preface

⚡⚡

Frigid Embrace is a historical commentary on the character of human culture in Alaska and how it has affected the natural environment there. Environmental historians have argued that a place shapes the people who live in it, and that the people shape the place where they are living. Most writers employing this concept focus on the geographical or biological environment. But the ideas a society has about the appropriate relationship between its members and the environment they live in, and depend on, become themselves a cultural shaping force. My study of Alaska history has persuaded me that while most Alaska residents have impressed their notion of what Alaska should be on the landscape they inhabit, they have been much less shaped themselves by that same landscape, much less than might be expected of a people who have migrated to America's last wilderness. While they have professed love for that wilderness and its arresting awe, beneath the surface of their perceptions they have remained immune from its power and majesty. They have been insensitive to their impact on nature and landscape, regarding the land as infinitely renewable and its resources as inexhaustible, and theirs to appropriate for their own uses.

Their activities seem to suggest that most non-Native Alaskans who migrated to Alaska did so with one primary thought in mind: to acquire wealth that could be transferred to more ostensibly hospitable climes. Alaska has always had a very high non-Native transiency rate and this is one of the indications of its colonial character. Considering themselves non-permanent residents, non-Native Alaskans generally have been much more concerned to extract wealth through commodification of the environment than to construct an identity that reflects the environment. While accumulating wealth, or trying to, most non-Natives helped to establish or lived in towns, and now cities; for the most part they have not inhabited the wilderness. In the towns they built, they set out to replicate the material, institutional, and ideological culture they left behind, much like the settlers of the earlier American West. Most Alaskans have been willing to stay in the territory only if they could enjoy the amenities and comforts of modern American culture. They did not go to the frontier to live a subsistence lifestyle in the wilderness. They went there for the money.

Most Alaskans have seen Alaska as the frontier. The idea of frontier depends on its opposite: development. If the wilderness is not developed, it's still wilderness—a denial of the purpose of frontier settlement. The conclusion of this study is that, throughout their history, Alaska's non-Native people, today 85 percent of the population, have treated the environment in which they live as a challenge to economic development. Despite their professions of sensitivity to, even love for, that environment, they have altered it insistently wherever they found economic benefit in doing so. They have viewed their impact on the land as light chiefly because there is so much of it. They have been convinced their activities are or can be made compatible with wilderness values.

Alaska is a colonial economy: its people do not produce what they consume, and what they do produce, primarily oil and fish, they consume only in minute quantities. Even the agricultural products they consume come from outside the region, for economies of scale defeat profitable agriculture within it. The only means through which a modern economy can be constructed in Alaska is through extraction of natural resources. But this requires extensive capital, more than resides in the region. It must, therefore, come from "Outside" Thus, the capability to replicate modern American material culture creates a significant dependence on absentee capital investment, investment over which the regional population can have but minimal influence. This circumstance, while not unique in the American West, is exacerbated in Alaska by an extreme level of dependence on extraction of a single resource. Today it is petroleum; in the past it has been gold, salmon, and copper. Such dependence increases anxiety about job security and continued residence in the state, and contributes to a "frontier mentality" that views undeveloped environment as a competitor and wilderness as an enemy.

Historically, the federal government has aided absentee capital investors in the development of the West's resources. Nowhere has this been more true than in Alaska. Federal expenditures nurtured economic development, aided non-Native settlement, and helped protect the Native population while implementing an aggressive program of acculturation. However, from the beginning of the twentieth century, Congress also moved to protect certain Alaska lands from exploitation, establishing such important conservation preserves as Mt. McKinley National Park, Glacier Bay National Monument, and the Arctic National Wildlife Refuge. And the federal government moved in the modern era to protect Alaska's Native people when, in the pursuit of economic development, the dominant non-Native people of the state proved willing to subordinate Native claims to such development. Thus, the federal government pursued multiple objectives in Alaska, supporting economic development in some areas, inhibiting it in others. Often, those multiple goals have been greatly at odds. As in other parts of the American West, settlers in Alaska have depended on the federal government, but have resented the government presence in their midst and their dependence on it. They have particularly resented any action of the government to restrict economic development.

The colonial character of Alaska's society and economy, together with the remote nature of the region and dependence on a single natural resource, have, I believe, exacerbated an oppositional tendency in the thinking of people isolated from the seats of their culture. Tensions between Native and non-Native people, between development-minded settlers and environmental protection, between federal and territorial or state government, between various localities within the region, and between global market forces and a conviction of a right to autonomy have been constant in Alaska's history. They are commonplace today. That the two most significant of these oppositions have been between Natives and non-Natives, and between settlers and environment, is the principal thesis of this study.

Though they characterize all of the region's history, those tensions are manifested particularly in Alaska's recent development. Modern Alaska, since World War II and statehood, has been dramatically, comprehensively shaped by the Alaska Native Claims Settlement Act of 1971 (ANCSA) and the Alaska National Interest Lands Conservation Act of 1980 (ANILCA). Probably the history of no other region of the United States has been so thoroughly determined by just two acts of Congress. Together they circumscribed land disposal, Native rights, conservation of resources, patterns of settlement, the realization of statehood, and the region's economic development. This work examines the impact of these acts on Alaska culture, their relationship to Alaskans' oppositional mode of thinking, and how they have shaped the relationship between nature and culture in Alaska.

I conceive of this work as a historical commentary. Habits of mind cannot be proven with satisfaction. Motivation and rationalization are often personal, and often malleable. Nonetheless, reactions and expressions, habits of behavior and thought, can provide clues to community thinking. At the same time, the work rests on the reconstructive work of a number of historians, as well as my own. I have sought to meld their work into the common theme of frontier opposition to Natives and environment.

Finally, because I want this work to be accessible to the general reader, I have not explicitly analyzed the theories of dependency, frontier, transiency, or environmental ethics. I have, however, referenced a number of the major historians I have relied on. I have tried not to take their conclusions out of context, nor distort them.

Acknowledgments

I wish to thank Bill Lang, series editor, for his encouragement throughout the preparation of this study. His understanding that modern Alaska constitutes a significant modern story about nature and culture, and that I could tell it, was a continuing comfort and inspiration throughout. My friend Bill Robbins has consistently sought to understand where Alaska "fits in," as his inclusion of it in conferences and collections attests. Much more important, my career as historian and scholar would be a pale reflection of whatever it is without his ever-present support and friendship.

Morgan Sherwood died on Hallowe'en, 2000. He was an unfailingly intelligent advocate of Alaska history, and a dear friend. The void left by his departure will not be filled. Morgan knew of his approaching death from cancer, and took care to vote absentee in the November election in California. It reminded him, he said, of the man who wanted to be buried in former mayor Richard J. Daley's Chicago, so he could remain politically active.

The scholar of northern Canada, Ken Coates, has worked for decades, along with Bill Morrison, to reorient northern studies away from comforting mythology and toward rigorous analysis. I hope this study will contribute to their efforts.

John Strohmeyer's arrival on the UA Anchorage campus in 1987 brought a new, shrewd perception to the analysis of modern Alaska, always expressed with insistent candor. I am indebted to the model he presents of accessible, honest writing, and clear thinking.

Mina Jacobs, dear friend and the most professional of archivists I thank for her abiding, reliable help at the Anchorage Museum of History and Art, and Caedmon Liburd of the UAA History Department for his support and commitment. And great thanks to Jo Alexander of Oregon State University Press for her careful and helpful counsel.

Introduction

Alaska History and Opposition

⊱⊰

Alaska has been a powerful force in American cultural imagination throughout the twentieth century. Until the present generation, its most potent role was as America's "last frontier," the last vestige in America of the conquest of nature, a nature that included American Indians. As Americans have interpreted their history, as they expanded westward, they replaced wild nature with a tamed, cultivated, and safe landscape, processing nature's wasted—i.e., unused—resources into the tools and materials of democratic and capitalist opportunity and wealth. Alaska was the last chapter in that westering saga.

In the last thirty years, however, Alaska's role in American national consciousness has changed dramatically. It is no longer the "last frontier"; it has become America's "last wilderness." Americans have determined that some of Alaska's last, vast untrammeled land should be preserved in perpetuity, protected from development and passed on to future generations in its present form, as natural landscape, and wherever possible, as wilderness. In other words, resources that were once seen as an

Valdez Glacier; Alaska as "last wilderness."
(Courtesy Anchorage Museum of History and Art)

impediment to progress now have become prized objects of respect and adulation, America's environmental crown jewels.

This change in Alaska's role for the nation reflects a fundamental change in the nation itself. Today, virtually no economic development project can be undertaken without a nod to environmental impact, no matter how superficial that nod may be. Yet, as Alaska was the last chapter in the saga of westward expansion, the sense of that saga is particularly strong in the state. And thus Alaska may be more conflicted over environmental protection than other places in America.

The new national environmental concern impacted Alaska society directly and continues to reverberate across the region, manifest particularly in politics and economy. In the 1960s, U.S. natural resource policy evolved from conservationism to environmentalism. Under conservationism, governments managed national and state lands by a multiple use policy, which emphasized commodification of those resources. New environmental policies mandated assessments of environmental impacts on a variety of land uses, sought to guarantee clean air and water, and protected endangered species, among others. More visionary measures set aside one hundred million acres of national public domain in the U.S. as wilderness, in both existing and new conservation units★, and provided for stricter controls on non-wilderness lands in such units. This legislation was put in place remarkably swiftly between 1960 and 1976.

Environmentalism came to Alaska in the monumental Alaska Native Claims Settlement Act (ANCSA) of 1971 and its companion Alaska National Interest Lands Conservation Act (ANILCA) of 1980. The latter established 104 million acres of new conservation units in Alaska, and designated 50 million acres as wilderness, half of the nation's total. ANILCA also mandated a rural subsistence use preference in Alaska, to guarantee that Alaska Natives would have access to fish, game, and other resources they depend upon. Many analysts regard the act as the most important environmental legislation in the nation's history. Upon leaving office, former President Jimmy Carter said it was the legislation during his presidency of which he was most proud.

ANILCA removed from potential development 28 percent of Alaska's total land base, and markedly increased the presence of the federal government in the state. Fifty-four million acres of federal conservation units had existed before ANILCA; now 42 percent of Alaska was reserved

---

★A conservation unit is a federal reservation of land in order to preserve it in its natural state; different sorts of reserves—parks,, refuges, wilderness areas—provide different degrees of protection.

from development to one degree or another. Alaska's senior U.S. Senator, Ted Stevens, has called ANILCA the worst Alaska legislation in the nation's history. Most Alaskans would likely agree, though the 85 percent of Alaskans who are non-Native immigrants are not united in their opposition to the subsistence and other provisions of ANILCA, any more than the 15 percent of indigenous heritage are united in support.

The state legislature has steadfastly refused for over twelve years to enact legislation to bring the state into compliance with ANILCA's subsistence provisions. The state constitution declares that the state's natural resources are to be enjoyed equally by all its citizens. Those state legislators who hold to a strict states' rights view have prevented the question of bringing the state into compliance from being presented to the voters as a referendum. Their refusal led in 1998 and 1999 to a federal takeover of fish and game management on federal and adjacent lands within the state; in other states, state agencies administer most federal land. Many, probably most Alaskans interpret ANILCA as an unfair, even immoral, environmental appropriation of the state's resources. Most non-Native Alaskans are aggressive defenders of states' rights. Whether ANILCA reduces economic potential in Alaska is a debatable point. The Alaska delegation in Congress succeeded in protecting areas known to have development potential by writing numerous management exceptions into the act; recent analysis has also suggested that the tourism value of resources in certain conservation areas may be greater in the long run than whatever short-term gain might be realized from their development.

But there is dismay in Alaska over environmentalism. Many in the state feel they may have embarked on a fool's errand. For many Alaskans understand themselves to be a part of the national saga of the frontier, the conquest of nature. That saga was characterized by struggle, for nature was a formidable foe, demanding, often threatening, frequently ruthless. But through sacrifice, determination, and ingenuity the conquerors prevailed. The removal of the Native people of the continent was a necessary part of this story; but Natives were ancillary to the story. The conquest would be complete when the new settlers would stand independent of outside support, of reliance on the Native people and, as much as possible, from nature itself.

The full development of this tale of national origins and destiny, the triumph of the American way, was completed in the contiguous states in the last half of the nineteenth century. Economically, completion of the transcontinental railroads, which more fully facilitated the practical integration of the West's resources into the world market stream and sped the distribution of industrial products back into the West, signaled the final conquest of the region. Politically, the granting of statehood symbolized the completion of the saga. With statehood, the citizen-settlers of the West achieved equality with their brethren in the more settled East.

In reality, the process was not complete. Western legislators were always outnumbered in Congress. And the West could not become economically independent, for the settlers demanded a modern standard of living, one characterized by profit and material consumption, but until World War II, most of the goods consumed in the West were made in the East. Moreover, the only basis for a modern economy in the West was the extraction of natural resources, which required industrial development, but the necessary capital did not exist in the West. Its infusion from eastern investors contributed to western dependence, as did the need to export most of the West's resources out of the region for processing. Subsidization of settlement and economic development by the federal government—in the form of geographic exploration, removal of the Indians, protection on the overland trails, dredging of western watercourses, land grants to the transcontinental railroads, and a host of other encouragements— also contributed to western dependence.

But dependence was not the American story. As historian Joyce Appleby has shown, the ideology of republican independence was quickly converted in Jeffersonian America into an embrace of capitalist individualism. The freedom to make profit became the engine of American democracy. Thus, personal independence became as central to American culture as collective independence and self-direction was to the national identity. In his 1893 essay on the significance of the frontier in American history, Frederick Jackson Turner argued that the dramatic struggle with nature on the frontier had created the distinctive American character of individualism and self-reliance, which differentiated American culture from those of its European antecedents. Such symbols of independence and rugged individualism as the cowboy and expansive western landscapes have served ever since to evoke the national saga of the conquest of western nature as the origin of American culture and character.

The culmination of this story developed just at the time the U.S. acquired Alaska and, to the degree that writers noticed Alaska at all, the new territory was quickly linked with the conquest saga. Alaska's role was to serve as a latter-day example of the process. Nature presented herself there in some of her most awesome and intimidating guises: cold, dark, snow-covered, volcanic, tectonic, and sparsely peopled. Above all,

Alaska was north, and thus a region of awe and mystery. To carry the tale to completion in so awesome and formidable a place, inhabitants would need to be at their most courageous, daring, and determined. Acknowledging the hostility of the northern environment, writers gave grudging respect to the Native people, particularly the Eskimos, who had lived and sustained themselves in that land and climate for centuries. But neither the writers nor the settlers respected the Natives' rights to their land and their culture, which, the conquerors assumed, must ultimately yield before the example of civilization.

So Alaska entered the national imagination as the final chapter in the story of the American West, the last frontier. Three waves of non-Native settlers migrated to the region, the first during the gold rush, the next during World War II and the Cold War, and the most recent in the 1970s, associated with construction of the oil pipeline and development of North Slope oil deposits. They went there to act out for the last time the central creation story of American culture. They would subdue and cultivate nature, and in the struggle establish American culture, and shape their own personal independence. The symbolic culmination of their adventure would be the same as in the continental states: statehood. By providing a greater degree of self-governance, settlers believed, statehood would improve opportunities for economic development.

Many of the old-fashioned historians who examined the historical record of the development of Alaska from the purchase in 1867, and particularly in the twentieth century, found much to confirm this story. There was little non-Native population in Alaska until the gold rush era at the turn of the twentieth century. The intrepid argonauts who hiked the Klondike trail and dispersed into the vast Alaska interior seemed the embodiment of rugged individualism. Those few who struck it rich became beholden to no one, masters of their own fate. Those who stayed established new towns, elected representatives to the congressionally authorized territorial legislature, sent an elected, non-voting representative to the U.S. Congress, and looked ahead to the day when statehood would establish their civic equality and confirm their American character.

But statehood was long in coming. There were a number of reasons. First, the population did not grow. The number of non-Natives in the territory from 1900 to 1940 was virtually the same, about thirty thousand, about the same as the Native population. That was insufficient for the tax base necessary to support statehood. Second, spokespersons for the most lucrative absentee investment in the territory, the canned salmon industry, fought statehood vigorously, expecting it would bring increased taxation and regulation. Third, the question of Native land title loomed, for, unlike the contiguous states, that title had not been formally extinguished, except in several conservation reserves set aside by the Congress before World War II. Fourth, conservation interest in the territory grew significantly during the Progressive period. The Tongass and Chugach National Forests were established before 1910, Mt. McKinley National Park in 1917, Katmai National Monument in 1918, after the 1912 eruption near there, and Glacier Bay National Monument in 1925. In addition, Congress set aside National Petroleum Reserve No. 4 on the central North Slope in 1923. Many national figures who took an interest in Alaska expected that additional federal withdrawals would be made in the territory.

The long delay in statehood confirmed the frontier character of the territory. The permanent settlers chafed, as the citizens of all the western territories had chafed, under the congressional rule characteristic of territorial status. Congress could disallow enactments of the territorial legislature; the territorial delegate to Congress did not have a vote. In addition, Congress maintained a host of substantive limitations on self-governing power, such as retention of authority over the management of fish and game resources. Municipal bonded indebtedness had to be approved by the Congress and was limited to 2 percent of assessed property valuation. During World War II and the early stages of the Cold War, residents had to obtain territorial resident identification cards, "green cards," from the Immigration and Naturalization Service to enter and leave the territory. Clearly, by the post-war period, such cumbersome, restrictive territorial governance was outmoded and unjustified.

Continuance of the territorial system suspended completion of Alaska's pioneer history, and the final act in the national historic westering saga. Paradoxically, Congress could not convey statehood until Alaskan culture more closely resembled American culture generally. The original reason for the territorial system had been to prevent irresponsible government by migrants whose primary interest in the West was not the construction of a new society, but their own aggrandizement. Territorial status shaped institutions and culture into familiar forms, consistent with national institutions and ideas. So writers before statehood celebrated the strides Alaskans had made toward the establishment of American culture in the north, often arguing defensively that Alaskans were as capable of self-government, as responsible and patriotic, and as committed to civic development, as people anywhere else in America, and certainly to the same degree as other citizens had been when they were granted statehood. And these writers chastised Congress for failing to honor this Alaskan achievement by conferring full "home rule."

The realities of Alaska's past were quite consistent with the history of the American West. From soon after the 1867 purchase of Alaska, investors across the country and from other countries gambled that the quantity and value of the region's natural resources would surpass the enormous costs involved in extracting a profit from their development. Until World War II, the only economy in the territory was generated by absentee investment first in gold, then in the salmon industry, and later in copper. At the same time, the federal government generously subsidized the settler culture, stepping in to assist when the costs of development overwhelmed private efforts, later moving to regulate monopolistic investors so as to preserve the democratic character of the new society. These sources sustained Alaska's thirty thousand non-Natives in the period between the Klondike gold rush and 1940. Then, with World War II, as in the rest of the American West, military and other federal spending supplanted industrial capitalization of resource extraction as the basis of the modern economy. In Alaska, this phase of economic development lasted until 1970, when oil development was added to government spending as the region's economic foundation.

But as in the history of the rest of the West, many non-Native settlers who moved to Alaska before statehood in 1959, and many who came afterward, as well, started north with the notion that they were latter-day pioneers with a last chance to participate in the frontier saga. The paradigm they carried with them was essentially imitative: they were going to do what had been done before—to establish their personal independence through self-reliant hard work, building a new, democratic society. Like their earlier models, they were motivated in part by a strong sense of mission, but by now many shared the belief that something had gone wrong in America, that the dream of individual self-sufficiency had been corrupted, primarily by government restrictions and bureaucracy. Only by leaving America, they thought, going to a place as yet undeveloped and uncorrupted by government, could they live out the old American dream. In this, they considered themselves different from their brethren in the states. In truth, they resembled latter-day Puritans in their determination to demonstrate how to build a "proper" society. They did not recognize the irony that congressional legitimization of the new society they intended to build could come only when they had demonstrated sufficient imitation of the culture they fled that Congress would have no anxiety regarding their "normalcy." Nor did they, any more than did their models in the older American West, recognize that the society they wished to build, and did build, was possible only through the classic method of absentee investment capital in natural resource extraction, supported by generous, continuing federal subsidy. The fact that the capital came from outside the region created dependence, a condition that western settlers routinely denied, and which is still poorly understood in popular culture today.

⊱⊰

Modern historians and others writing about Alaska have often emphasized the region's exceptionalities, and not without reason, for Alaska's natural environment is unique. Alaska is vast; it has the greatest expanses of wilderness land in the United States. Cold, long, dark, snowy winters are aspects of a climate that can appropriately be called harsh, under certain circumstances, brutal. Alaska has a particular cultural uniqueness as well, for the state's population is more culturally diverse than most places in America. Tribes from two major Indian groups live there—Athabaskan and Pacific Northwest Coast Indians, and two groups of non-Indian aboriginal people: Eskimos and Aleuts. Alaska has a higher number of Native Americans as a percentage of the total population than any other U.S. state. There are 211 designated Native villages in Alaska, and 227 federally recognized tribes. Of the total population of 626,000, 100,000 are Alaska Natives, 16 percent. At the same time, Alaska's non-Native population was, and remains, highly transient.

But, as suggested, these exceptionalities mask a fundamental replication of American culture in Alaska. Alaska's social, economic, political, and cultural commonalities with the states of the American West are so many that the region can be said to be culturally a part of that West. Most of its population is urban; 70 percent are concentrated in towns and cities along the southeast and south-central coasts, and along a rail corridor stretching inland from Seward on the Gulf of Alaska to Fairbanks in the interior. These communities are and always have been virtually indistinguishable from communities elsewhere in the United States. They consist of commercial establishments and office buildings, houses, condo and apartment structures, schools, universities, churches and hospitals, platted subdivisions, paved streets, parks, people, automobiles, and all the detritus of modern civilization: community government and organizations, civic institutions, service clubs, and traffic and congestion, noise, pollution, and "city hall." The people work for wages and salaries; like nearly everyone else in America they are dependent for their economic livelihood on decisions made by corporate managers and banking officers in places far from their homes and by people over whom they have little influence. Yet like many people across America they tend either not to know or to ignore these facts. They are more likely to be convinced that they are independent and self-reliant, adopting easily the mythology of the frontier West that is held so tenaciously by residents of the region from Omaha to Redding.

Canadian historian Ken Coates has written that we cannot understand northern settled places best by seeing them as exceptional. Virtually all of their citizens have reproduced the mainstream, settled-region's culture that characterized the places they came from. Rather, he has argued, documented commonalities among these communities provide a more useful starting point for analysis of their histories and characters. Some of these might include relationship with the "Outside," the nature of their internal politics, and their sociocultural and structural characteristics. He suggests two comparative criteria: remoteness and opposition. (Remoteness works better even than nordicity, Coates argues, for there are many remote places that are not northern.)

What are the unique qualities of remoteness? First, Coates suggests, there is the sense of being outside the mainstream, outside the centers and sources of culture. Since remote communities, increasingly even Native communities, take their values from these external centers, their leaders' expressions of community identity and collective goals often appear defensive. When the institutions and norms of the settled regions are finally put in place, community leaders announce their arrival with a mixture of pride and relief. Thus, every new hospital, community center, and choral society, every new government department, every new commercial outlet elicits proclamations of normality and progress.

It is not only Alaska's culture that is defined by outside forces. The same is true of the economy, which today is dominated by extraction of a single natural resource: petroleum. Oil has transformed Alaska. It is the foundation of the state's modern economy: jobs, business, government revenue, and spending, all sectors of the economy benefit from their dependence on oil production. The oil industry paid about $50 billion in taxes to the State of Alaska between 1977 and 2000. It would be difficult to overdramatize the significance of oil production to Alaska since 1970. Without it, the non–Native population of the region would be much less; there would be fewer jobs, and a much smaller regional ancillary economy. Oil dependence in Alaska is a major theme in this study. The oil industry remade Alaska, and continues to do so. But Alaska residents had very little to do with that transformation, either its origins or its structure. The pipeline project was facilitated only through

Congress's passage of the Native claims settlement act and, later, direct congressional authorization of construction.

Economic dominance from outside the region is accompanied by outside political control, manifest most powerfully in the presence and activities of the federal government. In Alaska, for example, the federal government holds title to 228 million acres of land, 60 percent of Alaska's landbase, an area more than twice as large as California; 154 million acres are in conservation and strategic mineral reserves, and 74 million acres are unassigned public domain, a portion of which is also designated wilderness. In addition, since federal power is constitutionally superior to state sovereign power, the federal government's role in land and resource development is substantial. An additional 44 million acres are owned by regional and village Native corporations.

Federal and Native ownership of large blocs of land in Alaska, together with substantial control of the region's economic survival by the oil industry, conflict with Alaskans' expectations of independence. The presence of so much federally owned and protected land, and the large bureaucracy responsible for it, challenges Alaskans' notions of their destiny, for most still believe the land should be "opened up," i.e., made to serve economic development. The Alaska Native Claims Act of 1971 (ANCSA) and the 1980 Alaska National Interest Lands Conservation Act (ANILCA) both significantly influence life in the state because they so directly define the opportunities for and character of economic development. Collectively their provisions impact 72 percent of Alaska's vast land area, whose resources hold the only potential for future economic development.

Many Alaskans, perhaps most, have chafed mightily under federal sovereignty. Most non–Natives have come to Alaska poorly informed regarding the federal/state relationship articulated in the U.S. Constitution and adjudicated through two centuries of political development. Many confuse the moral right of self-governance with limitations on that right imposed by the federal constitution and membership in the federal union. Thus, they are surprised to discover that residence in Alaska does not guarantee control over the real estate and natural resources in the state. This partly explains how the atmosphere in which the Alaska lands act was debated in the late 1970s and passed in 1980 became highly charged and volatile in Alaska.

Over thirty years, congressional action has defined Alaska, and Alaskans generally resent Congress's proprietary role in their state. Nor surprisingly Alaskans are less resentful of corporate control of the economic conditions of their lives by the oil industry. The oil industry provides jobs and supports the ancillary economy; the federal government also provides jobs but in addition threatens to prevent the creation of new ones and perhaps even reduce the number already existing through land withdrawals. So it easily becomes an agent of villainy for Alaskans. But development in Alaska today and in the future will continue to depend, as it has historically depended, on investment of private capital from outside the region and cooperative development strategies by the federal government. Alaskans joke about the future of their state being determined in the boardrooms of British Petroleum in London and Phillips Petroleum in Bartlesville, Oklahoma. These corporate boards act in response to a variety of factors which may influence profit and development, in particular market forces. Thus, when the price of oil fell to less than $15 per barrel in 1985, producers in Alaska curtailed exploratory activity. When the price recovered to $25, and the industry received assurances of support from state government, British Petroleum and ARCO resumed exploratory work on Alaska's North Slope. In far northwest Alaska, on the Arctic Ocean coast, the world's largest known zinc deposit, called Red Dog and owned by the Canadian firm Cominco Mining, was discovered several decades ago. But development began only in the mid-1980s and production in 1989 because the world price of zinc would not support development until that time. In 1999 the mine produced $123 million worth of zinc. In the 1990s, two pulp mills operating in southeast Alaska, in the Tongass National Forest, closed down. These were the only pulp mills in Alaska. Though environmental factors contributed, the primary reason for the closures was the collapse of the pulp market. Such immediate dependence on forces beyond Alaskans' control exacerbates their sense of isolation and powerlessness.

Another feature of remote regions has to do with self-perception. People in remote regions often seem to deny their dependence on the "Outside." Alaskans who are by choice living physically outside the mainstream of American culture call people who are not Alaskans "Outsiders" and refer to the place where non-residents live as "Outside." Politicians frequently call for diversification of the regional economy, proposing unrealistic projects. Former Alaska Governor Steve Cowper, for example, urged that Alaska attempt to attract electronic banking and stock-trading firms and other cyberbusinesses whose physical locations are theoretically independent of their activities. The governor seemed to think that Alaska's unusual winter living conditions would not be an impediment to the personnel who work in those industries. Sometimes politicians assert more influence than they actually have over the federal government and distant corporation boards, and sometimes may act on their own naïve assumptions. In 1991, for example, Alaska Governor Walter Hickel's administration sued the U.S. in federal court for breach of contract, charging that passage of the Alaska native claims act in 1971 and the Alaska lands act in 1980 constituted a violation of Congress's statehood compact with Alaska, asking for $29 billion in compensation. As predicted by a number of constitutional lawyers, the judge dismissed the case, stating that a statehood compact cannot be analogized to a commercial contract, and that as federal sovereignty is superior to state sovereignty, Congress can amend its previous legislation as it deems necessary.

As Coates's analysis suggests, the power of the federal government in Alaska exacerbates greatly the sense of being outside the mainstream. Not only have Alaskans felt the federal presence in the 60 percent of the land base that is in federal ownership, but they have felt it, also, in regard to federal protection and representation of Alaska's Native people, and their distinct concerns. Alaska Natives, with all Native Americans, enjoy a special trust relationship with the federal government. The Alaska lands act manifested one aspect of that special relationship in the provision mandating a rural preference for subsistence hunting and fishing. The state's failure to provide for rural subsistence preference led the state's principal Native organization, the Alaska Federation of Natives, to resolve, in spring 2000, to rely on Congress and the federal government, rather than the state government, as previously, to fairly address the subsistence issue. Alaskans, then, have an acute sense of their relationship to and dependence on "Outside" forces, one which exacerbates their perception of difference.

Coates suggested another characteristic of remote settlements: intense internal political struggles. One such struggle is between Native and non-Native peoples, regions, and communities. Issues which have divided northern societies along racial lines include conflicting visions of land ownership, resource harvesting, and social policy. As noted above, the federal government has intervened to guarantee Native rights. Alaska manifests a long history of such intervention and Native empowerment. Other circumstances have empowered Alaska Natives, as well.

The federal government executed no treaties with Alaska Native people. Congress halted treaty making in 1871, just four years after the Alaska purchase; the only mention of Natives in the purchase treaty was a clause stating that the "uncivilized tribes" were to be "subject to such laws and regulations as the United States may, from time to time, adopt in regard to aboriginal tribes of that country." In the first civil government act for Alaska, in 1884, Congress elaborated on the relationship between Natives and non-Natives. The statute protected Indians "In the possession of any lands actually in their use or occupation." Native title to land in Alaska would not be fully clarified until the modern claims settlement act, in 1971.

The same 1884 legislation authorized the government to establish schools "without regard to race" wherever there were school-age children in the territory, a duty carried out by the U.S. Bureau of Education. (This did not mean, incidentally, that the schools were integrated; it meant that the government assumed a responsibility to provide schools where there were children, Native schools for Native children, white schools for white children.) The schools empowered Natives, both by imparting literacy, general knowledge, and some practical skills (i.e., acculturation) and by encouraging leadership. School personnel accepted, nay, celebrated, the concomitant suppression of traditional Native culture, and were naive or ambivalent on the question of racial equality. As we shall see in subsequent chapters, Alaska Natives early developed the capabilities to pursue their own objectives, and profited immensely from the absence of treaties, reservations, superintendencies, annuities, and dependence on the government for direct survival, a dependence often enough betrayed by the trustees in the contiguous states and territories.

There have been moments of cooperation between Alaska Natives and non-Natives: passage in the territorial legislature of an anti-discrimination act in 1945, the battle for statehood in the 1950s, the framing of the Native claims settlement between 1968 and 1971, and others. But there have also been many other moments of discord, distrust, and frustration, most recently over the guarantee of access to subsistence resources, the question of Native sovereignty, and the allocation of state funds for material infrastructures and to support economic sustainability in Native villages.

Access to subsistence resources is but part of a larger issue, connection to the land. Indigenous people not only have a permanent commitment to residence in the state, but are rooted to the land, both as a homeland and as provider of daily resources. In most of Alaska's 211 Native villages, many people could not get by without reliance on subsistence, for fish and for game. The contrast is extreme between their sense of identification with the land, and the attitudes of short-term periodic oilfield workers whose commitments lie far outside Alaska and whose livelihoods depend on commodification of the land. But the social structure is more complicated, for the indigenous people who live in the vicinity of

Prudhoe Bay, where they have created a municipal government which permits them to tax oil production, support the commodification of these resources. The Athabaskan Indians, living several hundred miles away, but dependent upon caribou herds that migrate through lands adjacent to the oil patch, fear such commodification, and the development which accompanies it. This is only one of the tensions among Native groups in the state.

In his history of the American West, Richard White identified three types of westward migration: community, utopian, and modern. The first two types of migrants went West to stay, either to build a new but replicated society from a base of kinship or former acquaintance, or to build a wholly new kind of society, with alternative values, such as the Mormons. The third type, increasingly important in the later history of the West, comprised the individuals who went to get rich and then transfer their new worth back to more settled regions. Coates suggests that another important struggle in remote regions is that between permanent and transient residents. Newcomers, Coates asserts, always outnumber permanent residents, and greatly outnumber the indigenous population.

There has not been much study of transiency in Alaska. Analysts recognize that it may be manifest in political commitment—or lack of it—and social programs, but disagree on the nature and degree of its impact. Transients may not participate in politics at all, judging that they know too little. Or if they do participate they may favor candidates who endorse short-term policies with immediate benefits, such as low taxation and a refusal to pass bond issues or zoning ordinances, over longer term measures that might call for greater sacrifice. Transience seems to have been an accepted aspect of the northern experience in Alaska. In a series of oral history interviews of people who had lived in Anchorage before 1940 and were still there in 1996, several respondents, including a newspaper editor and a noted civic leader, spoke without malice or bitterness of employing the talents and financial contributions of "short termers." On the other hand, most respondents acknowledged the potential negative effects for long-term community goals of a highly transient population.

The rate of transience has declined slightly in the most recent years in Alaska as production at the Prudhoe Bay oil field has passed its peak, and there is no new economic boom on the horizon. But it is still high, and rapid turnover in public- and private-sector jobs is the norm. Anecdotal evidence suggests that the tension between community and modern migrants is not substantial in Alaska; people seem focused on the demands of the present, with little historical perspective, and little vision of the future.

⊱⊰

Coates's analysis of all of these factors led him to conclude that northern settlements are characterized by a culture of opposition. Struggles between indigenous and non-indigenous peoples, between transient and permanent residents, between the region and the nation, between the desire to control the development of their natural resources and the realities of the global market, and finally, between popular culture and the realities of northern economies seem to preoccupy northern residents. They have certainly preoccupied Alaska. These oppositions are rooted in the regions' histories, and are perpetuated and exacerbated by contemporary influences. They have been internalized, Coates suggests, into a culture of antagonism. Opposition has generated a regional consciousness built on a sense of grievance that is usually ill founded. It has made northern populations vulnerable to political manipulation, both from without and within. And it has contributed to an inflated sense of regional importance. It has been, Coates argues, a barrier to development and has been intensely destructive of community bonds and the generation of a positive, supportive culture.

Coates's analysis seems to fit Alaska well. The inconsistencies in Alaskans' views of themselves and their history, the confusion regarding Native culture and legitimacy, the high transiency rate, and the dependence on global, absentee investment are all consistent with Coates's characterization of other northern and remote places. In the following pages we will examine Alaska's history in light of this analysis, with the hope of understanding more fully the nature of Alaska's society.

Two oppositions in Alaska's history, however, claim pride of place as preoccupations for Alaskans. The first is between indigenous and non-indigenous people. Today Alaska Natives are perhaps more empowered than any other groups of Native Americans, yet distrust between Native and non-Native residents is potent. Historically, Alaska Natives suffered significant discrimination. They achieved economic and political parity only with the passage of the Native claims settlement act in 1971, and while that parity has produced substantial social equity today, it is hardly complete and cannot be taken for granted, as is manifest in statistics dealing with the criminal justice system, and with sexual crimes and abuse.

The other opposition is that directed at environmentalism, and restrictions, primarily federal, on current land use and potential future development in Alaska. Today, most Alaskans favor congressional action to open a portion of the Arctic National Wildlife Refuge to oil exploration, and should oil be found, development. Most people in the nation apparently do not, though the majority view on the issue seems somewhat related to the price of gasoline. Alaskans have attacked federal conservation and environmental actions through most of the region's history. Federal policy on game, on fish, on migratory mammals and waterfowl, federal creation of conservation areas such as Mt. McKinley and Glacier Bay, and the creation by the Alaska lands act of vast wilderness areas in Alaska have consistently been vilified and resisted. Only in their reaction to the *Exxon Valdez* oil spill in 1989 have Alaskans seemed broadly supportive of measures to restrain development in the name of environmental protection. With other Americans, Alaskans profess concern for the environment. But a majority of state politicians, as well as spokespeople for commercial and financial interests, argue that industry can develop Alaska's resources without damage to the environment. Such groups as the Resource Development Council, the Alaska Miners' Association, the Alaska Loggers Association, and the Alaska Chamber of Commerce, together with the predictable Alaska Oil and Gas Association and the development giants British Petroleum and Phillips Petroleum, assert that ANWR, for example, can be drilled with no significant alteration of the land or its resources. In this they are supported by those Inuit people who have municipal governmental jurisdiction over existing North Slope development and who control part of ANWR. Alaskan leaders supported the Atomic Energy Commission's nuclear test regime on Amchitka Island in the 1960s, and that same agency's planned use of low-yield nuclear devices to create an artificial harbor on Alaska's western Arctic coast in the 1950s. They supported the U.S. Army Corps of Engineers' 1950s plan to construct a massive hydroelectric dam on the Yukon River. They supported construction of the trans-Alaska pipeline, and vigorously and vociferously opposed the Alaska lands act. They supported opening the Tongass National Forest to timber lease sales in 1947 despite protests by Tlingit-Haida Indians who had an active land claim for the area before U.S. courts. And in the 1980s they loudly protested reforms to the Alaska lands act which, when passed in 1990, reduced the annual federal subsidization of lease sales on that forest and reduced the mandated annual number of board-feet to be cut. Not all Alaskans took anti-environmental positions on these issues, but most did. And in every case, opponents argued that environmental concerns were overstated and alarmist.

Writing in the *Anchorage Daily News* on the eve of the millennium celebration, editorial page editor Michael Carey wrote that several themes ran through Alaska history in the twentieth century. He chose the paradigm "tension" to express them. There had been, he wrote, "tensions with the federal government," which expressed themselves in battles over land use, resource management, the question of statehood, and federal obligations to Natives. To many Alaskans, Carey wrote, Washington "is still the distant, careless landlord." There were as well, he wrote, "tensions with Outside interests." Alaska has been "a resource colony to generations of Outside investors." Long before the oil industry showed serious interest in the north, the great Alaska fortunes were in Seattle, San Francisco, New York, and other stateside cities. The statehood movement was in good measure, Carey wrote, a rebellion against the canned salmon interests and mining companies that "refused to leave a nickel in Alaska." Outside capital has long been sought, but feared. Politicians' frequent outbursts against environmentalists also have their roots in Alaskans' traditional fear of the power of Outsiders over their lives.. Finally, Carey wrote, there were "tensions between regions and races." Alaska Natives' assertion of their rights, and their growing economic power in the state following the Alaska Native Claims Settlement Act of 1971, have "not always been greeted with enthusiasm by their non-Native neighbors."

Carey's was an astute analysis of Alaska's history. Born in Alaska and raised in the bush and in Fairbanks, Carey spoke from the perspective of fifteen years of editorial work at the state's largest circulation newspaper. His conclusions were remarkably consistent with Coates's theoretical analysis. In the following pages we shall examine these oppositions in Alaska history, especially the issues of indigenous rights and environmental protection. While they are not unique to Alaska in content, they may be quite unique in magnitude, and in their history. But Alaskans do not recognize the historical character of these issues and the oppositional stance their predecessors have taken toward them; they are not well educated about the history of the region and the high transiency rate mitigates against historical understanding. Thus, most Alaskans miss the historical context, which gives force to Native reactions to contemporary policies which disadvantage Natives to the benefit of urban Alaskans. A per capita redistribution of state education funds in accord with population increases in urban Alaska, for example, reminds Native Alaskans of the long history of educational discrimination. Not realizing that the issue is not new condemns modern Alaskans to failure to appreciate its depth of meaning.

By the same token, ignorance of the realities of the federal/state relationship, together with lack of understanding of the rise of environmentalism and the history of conservation withdrawals in Alaska, condemns Alaskans perpetually to fight on the wrong battleground, challenging "violations" of the "statehood compact." Most particularly, such ignorance condemns Alaskans to misunderstand the legitimacy and the origins of federal environmental regulations applied in the state. It is particularly important that each new generation of Alaskans have the opportunity to understand and assess the significance of the state's historical legacy, for only then can they bring an informed view to their participation in the shaping of public policy.

To the oppositional mode of thinking on these issues, I will add another in the following pages: greed. I will argue that the false notion of Alaska's history, together with the recent phenomenon of the Alaska Permanent Fund dividend program, has exacerbated the pattern of modern migration delineated by Richard White, migrants whose primary interest is not the creation of a society for their progeny, but self-aggrandizement, primarily economic self-aggrandizement. Oil production in Alaska has supported a high material standard of living for many more people than could be sustained by all other economic factors presently extant in the state combined. Distrust of government, partly a function of a jaundiced view of federal sustenance of Alaska and stemming partly from ignorance of the nature of the federal/state relationship under the U.S. Constitution, seems to have focused the attention of the citizenry on what they can get for themselves. The Alaska Permanent Fund dividend is a tangible benefit of being in Alaska, tangible in the year 2000 in the amount of nearly $2,000 per resident. Many citizens seem to agree with the writer of a letter to the editor of the state's largest newspaper, but one of many, who said "to the government: keep your hands off my dividend." That the dividend is generated by a taxing structure enacted by the state legislature and administered by the executive branch, and that the distribution of the earnings of the Fund as dividend to Alaska citizens was and is a program created and sustained by the legislature, seems not to have registered with this citizen.

We shall take up the story of Alaska's historical reality with the establishment of the first modern economy in the territory, thirteen years after the region's purchase by the United States in 1867.

1

A Good American Town

֍ ֍

In the winter of 1880-81, a modest town sprang suddenly to life along the edge of Gastineau Channel in Alaska's southeast panhandle. The previous summer, the steep, forested slopes of the rugged mountains along the channel had plunged undisturbed into its deep, blue waters. But by Christmas, a large swath of the forest had been cut, and a number of streets had been laid out, across whose muddy tracks businesses of every sort faced one another. Soon after, several large warehouses arose along a new waterfront, and ships from Seattle and San Francisco began to tie up with increasing frequency. The excitement of new enterprise was evident everywhere as buildings multiplied and people went eagerly about their appointed tasks. There was an air of exuberant determination about this creation; nothing appeared tentative or uncertain.

Most of the little town sat on a triangular, rising shelf at the water's edge, at the base of several huge mountains, their crests and valleys white with snow. By summer 1882 the community comprised scores of small tidy white-painted frame houses and numerous larger ones. Various commercial buildings now sat among the stumps of what obviously had been very large trees only shortly before, cedar, most likely, judging from the shake roofs on virtually every structure. The town already looked solid and well built, as if the residents and business owners intended to stay. Determinedly climbing the mountain slopes and spilling out into the ocean channel on piers driven into the seafloor, the town's appearance suggested vitality and impatience, as if the inhabitants could barely contain their energy and relish to build and to transform.

The town was Juneau, the seat of what had quickly become the territory's most significant economic enterprise, after discovery in 1880 of the Treadwell gold deposits on Douglas Island, a quarter mile across the channel. The Treadwell Mines exploited a substantial find of low-grade gold ore in veins running beneath the island and the adjacent channel. By 1885 the deposit supported one of North America's largest gold stamp mills and, by the turn of the century, the largest. Prospectors initially had found placer deposits on the Juneau side of the channel, on the mainland, then on Douglas Island; only later did they find the Treadwell lodes. The placers played out quickly, as usually happened with western gold strikes, though for several years they produced a half-million dollars worth of gold annually. But the Treadwell lodes, and smaller lodes found later on the mainland, had by 1890 generated six separate communities: Juneau, Thane, and the Auk (for the Auk tribe of Tlingit Indians) Native village on the mainland, and Treadwell, Douglas, and a sizeable Native village on Douglas Island. Together they were home to about two thousand people by 1890. Juneau was the largest, with 1,253 inhabitants, 671 of whom were whites. Three hundred Indians lived in the Native communities.

By 1890, Juneau was a fully modern community, despite its youth. The U.S. census reported that it was amply supplied with sidewalks, its main streets were graveled, and its stores completely stocked. A list of its primary businesses suggests the commercial character of the place: nine general merchandise houses, twenty-two saloons, three hotels, two separate restaurants, a boarding house, a hospital, three churches, a fire brigade, a brass band, two stove and tin ware shops, two jewelry stores, two breweries, two fur and curio shops, two cigar factories, a slaughterhouse, a meat market, a lumber mill, a weekly newspaper, a millinery shop, a photographer's studio, a confectionery, a steam laundry, a barber, and several blacksmith shops. There was also a collection of lawyers and doctors. A large theater, known as the "opera house," seated four hundred and was used for public meetings in addition to entertainments. Douglas was a smaller community, but nonetheless supported thirteen saloons, a drug store, four general merchandise stores, two grocery stores, two hotels, a barbershop, and a shoe shop. There was also a post office. Treadwell was a collection of mine buildings, including residence cottages for administrative staff. Thane was an aggregation of mine facilities for lode deposits on the Juneau side of the channel, with a few independent commercial establishments.

Taken together, these communities represented a substantial new departure in Alaska, the beginning of Alaska frontier settlement. It was a beginning that rested squarely on the exploitation of the Treadwell Mines. From a small lode deposit taken over from a prospector-turned-merchant who needed money to pay for inventory, San Francisco investors had developed the site into four distinct mines where muckers dug out thirty tons of ore daily. At the turn of the century, 880 crushing stamps roared day and night, pulverizing the low-grade rock. Amalgamation, using chlorination and mercury, extracted half the gold at Treadwell. The remainder was smelted from processed ore shipped to Tacoma, Washington. The work force at Treadwell exceeded two thousand; one company boarding house fed 480 men at a sitting. The investment in men and machines was massive for the time and place.

Most resident non-Native Alaskans, and many Natives, too, welcomed enthusiastically the Treadwell investment and the development of urban Juneau which it spawned, for before 1880 Alaska's developmental prospects had looked dim. The first decennial census in Alaska had been taken that year. The enumerator counted just 435 non-Natives in the whole territory. Though there has been some criticism of the counter's thoroughness, his number was in fact representative of the character of the territory at the time. Sitka, the old Russian capital, had boomed briefly at the time of the Alaska purchase, in 1867 and 1868. But by 1878 observers counted barely three hundred non-Natives, where in 1869 there had been upwards of one thousand. Several dozen white merchants struggled to survive there, supplying the Native boarding school run by the Presbyterian Board of Foreign Missions and, until 1877, a contingent of Army troops. But in that year the Army left, and Sitka's future turned even bleaker. There was nothing in Sitka from which to construct a sustaining economy: no significant gold had been discovered, the fur trade was concentrated elsewhere, mainly on the Pribilof Islands and in the interior, the forest industry would not be developed for nearly a century, nor a vigorous canned salmon industry for a decade. And with no economy to provide profits for business owners and jobs for wage earners, there was no reason for non-Natives to stay, for they had not come for the joy of living a subsistence existence in far-north Sitka; they had come to make money.

Circumstances were much the same across the territory. A few merchants hung on in the old Russian towns of Kodiak and Unalaska. Wrangell, at the mouth of the Stikine River, had boomed some in 1872, merchants there selling supplies to miners in the newly discovered Cassiar gold district far up that river in northern British Columbia. But the Cassiar rush was short lived, and by 1879 Wrangell, too, had become a shadow of its recent past. Grass grew in its few formerly busy streets, and officials lamented that the only people now attracted north were the worst sort of "adventurers," a "God-abandoned, God-forsaken, desperate, and rascally set of wretches . . ."

In 1880 fewer than one hundred non-Native prospectors and trappers roamed Alaska's interior rivers taking marten, river otter, and black bear pelts for the modest fur market. Many were comfortably integrated into the Native culture of the region, intermarrying and adopting Native trading behaviors. The number of fur-bearers would not support a substantial harvest, for despite notions of inexhaustible resources, Alaska was lightly forested above 60°, and its landscapes did not support a large fur population. Across the rest of the territory, 32,000 Natives lived much as they had before the arrival of Europeans and Americans, with various alterations of traditional culture depending on the degree of occasional contact they had with American non-Natives. Where that contact was greatest, in the southeast panhandle, the Natives helped to sustain the meager white population by bartering deer and other game.

Ten years later Alaska had undergone a dramatic change. The non-Native population of the territory had increased tenfold. In addition to the explosive growth of Juneau, new prospectors were hurrying to the upper Yukon in the aftermath of a placer discovery on the Fortymile River. Sitka, named by Congress the territorial capital, had ceased its decline and had grown to over one thousand non-Natives, most of them employees of the federal government. In addition, a completely new industry had started: canned Pacific salmon. Investors had built thirty-seven canneries in Alaska by 1889. In 1895 Territorial Governor James Sheakley estimated the non-Native population to be eight thousand, most of it concentrated in Southeast, mostly in Juneau and its satellites.

What changed Alaska was the capital poured into the region by investors and, later, corporations seeking substantial profit in natural resource exploitation and willing to support major industrial development in pursuit of that profit. The Treadwell Mines, whose success built the city of Juneau, were named for an investment agent, John Treadwell, an experienced mining engineer and surveyor with experience in Nevada and California, who was sent to Alaska to assess potential investment opportunities. Treadwell didn't see much, but he took a chance on some lode deposits being sold by a prospector who had decided to go into the

Yupik dancer at a modern dance festival.
(Courtesy Anchorage Museum of History and Art)

grocery business and need money to pay for his inventory. That investment became the Treadwell Mines, which generated the economy that attracted the adventuresome north—but only to well-paying jobs.

Reflecting on this over a decade later, Juneau's then-mayor, George Forrest, understood clearly how it had happened. "Juneau was a placer mining town, the most transitory of human habitations," he wrote in the *Alaska Yukon Magazine*, and had it remained so, ". . . nothing would now remain to mark the place . . . save the remnants of a few old shacks. But "there was a destiny for the place much more enduring . . ." he continued, due to its location "in the midst of a country rich in its quartz deposits." Those gold-bearing deposits were most extensive on Douglas Island; in fact they seemed inexhaustible. As long as the resource lasted, the investors were happy to sustain Alaska. But in 1917, a major implosion of Gastineau Channel waters flooded the whole works, by then a warren of underground tunnels, shafts, stopes, and rails. Because the cost would have overwhelmed the return, the mines were never rebuilt. And without a profitable resource, the investors turned their attention elsewhere.

But in the early 1880s, Alaska's new population surge and the potential for more mineral lode finds caught the attention of potential investors across the country. Soon new money developed additional mines in Juneau, at the deposits on the mainland side of the channel, Alaska Perseverance, Alaska-Juneau, and Ebner, among them. Together, all the various mines on both sides of the channel, clinging brashly and confidently to the steep, forested mountain slopes, constituted a remarkable industrial complex, somewhat incongruous with the largely unaltered natural landscape in which they were situated, noisy, robust, active around the clock. By 1890 the value of the product shipped south every month from the Treadwell works alone was over $100,000. Congress reported that the gross value of the gold produced in 1887 was $2.5 million.

Patricia Nelson Limerick wrote in her history of the modern West, *The Legacy of Conquest: The Unbroken Past of the American West,* that the region's early economic development rested on a foundation of "furs, farmland, timber, minerals, and federal money," upon which settlers were dependent for their livelihoods. There would be no commercial farming in Alaska, but if fish be substituted for farmland, Limerick's observation fits Alaska as well. The new economy was wholly extractive, dependent on the outside capital which had started the development and which maintained the operation and its continuing expansion. Virtually nothing was produced in the town. Juneau was, in a loose sense, a company town, nearly completely dependent on monies the company dispensed. When, under what conditions, and how much money the company might dispense was not within the control of Juneau's residents. It was the result of decisions made by the investors and they would make those decisions in their own interests and those of their stockholders, not those of the people of Juneau.

Such dependence on outside forces was not unique or even unusual in the American West, as Limerick has indicated. But often the economies of individual towns in the West became somewhat diversified, and thus less dependent on a single enterprise or industry. They often became integrated into a more diversified regional economy, which also lessened their dependence on a single source of investment. This would not be the case in Alaska. Before the discovery of lode gold at Juneau, there was no economy which would attract or hold non-Natives, or which could facilitate the acculturation to economic individualism of those Natives who might wish that opportunity. Non-natives would go north only if they could expect to better their economic circumstances in so doing. No more than anywhere else in the American west, people did not go to this newly developing region to engage in subsistence living. They wanted sufficient discretionary income to acquire the goods and services which constituted a level of material well being Americans were growing used to, which was considerably more than subsistence. Nor did people coming to Alaska seek agricultural opportunities, and in any case, Alaska did not have them. With the exception of the few who went prospecting, immigrants to Alaska sought jobs, and the Treadwell development at Juneau was the first developmental surge in Alaska's history that provided them in appreciable numbers, and with the prospect of their being long-lived. So that is where people went.

The citizens of Juneau and the other towns that formed at the base of Alaska's southeast coastal mountains were well schooled in the basic principles of American political culture. The Alaska they came to in 1880 and 1881 violated those principles in a fundamental way: there was no civil government. Congress had sanctioned military occupation, but no military governor. Soon after they arrived in Alaska, the new non-Native residents addressed this situation. American citizens were not comfortable with the idea of military rule; it violated their democratic conviction that government should be based on the consent of the

Juneau, c. 1890. (Courtesy Anchorage Museum of History and Art)

governed. The Juneau business community called a political convention into being in 1881. The towns of Sitka and Wrangell each sent five delegates to join five from Juneau. The conventioneers drafted a petition to Congress calling for an organic act that would establish civil rule for Alaska. Before adjourning, they called for an election in Alaska in September to name a person to travel to Washington, D.C., to present their petition. U.S. Customs Collector Mottrom Ball was elected.

In addition, Alaska had acquired an aggressive lobbyist in Dr. Sheldon Jackson of the Presbyterian Board of Home Missions. Jackson first visited Alaska in 1877 and found it, from his point of view, a virtually untapped mission opportunity. At the time, the only representatives of Christianity were seventeen Russian priests spread across the territory. Jackson undertook a program of establishing Presbyterian day schools in as many Native villages as he could raise private funds to support. When other Christian denominations took a mission interest in the territory, Jackson counseled against direct competition, but even so they could reach only a small number of Alaska's more than two hundred Native communities. Jackson's response was to agitate for government funds to help. Embracing the idea of a comprehensive government program for Alaska, he urged Congress to adopt a traditional early civil government measure for Alaska, and add to it a permanent provision for funding Native education.

Two unusual circumstances aided Jackson's plan. First, there were no Indian reservations in Alaska, for the U.S. government had concluded no treaties with Alaska Natives. With no government annuity payments necessary for the self-sufficient and unrestricted Native population, the only requirement, Jackson argued, was funds for education. Jackson also had Presbyterian friends in the highest government circles, including President Benjamin Harrison in the White House and Commissioner John Eaton at U.S Bureau of Education in the Interior Department.

Responding to the changed circumstances in Alaska and to Sheldon Jackson's persistent lobbying campaign, Congress passed the first civil government act for Alaska in 1884. It provided for a governor and federal judge appointed by the president, and for several minor civil officials, such as marshals, court clerks, and the like. Preparatory to its passage, Congress ordered a number of reports on Alaska's resources and on its non-Native population. Generally, these fairly glowed with positive assessments of the territory's resources and its potential for development. Several leaders credited Jackson with passage of the act and Congress responded to Jackson's representations: the act included the somewhat unusual office of "General Agent of Education." The agent's responsibility was to "make needful and proper provision for the education of children of school age in the Territory of Alaska, without reference to race." The language on race did not represent an enlightened view of the equality of Alaska Natives or the ideal of an integrated society. Quite the opposite; it simply called upon the General Agent, a position in which Jackson would serve from 1885 to 1906, to establish schools where there were school-age children: Native schools in Native villages, separate Native and white schools in the white towns where there were both Natives and whites. Congress intended the provision to meet two obligations: provide federal support for economic development and non-Native settlement in Alaska and at the same time meet its acknowledged obligation to provide for the acculturation of Alaska's Native population.

But Congress and would-be investors were not interested primarily in Alaska's Native population. Exploitation of Alaska's resource potential was what attracted national attention. While waiting for new gold discoveries, investors hoped other potentially profitable Alaskan resources might be identified. Pacific salmon would be the next such resource.

The canned salmon industry began in California in 1864 and on the Columbia River after the Civil War. By 1886 there were fifty-five canneries on the Columbia, and entrepreneurs pushed north to the Fraser River in British Columbia, and to Alaska. The first cannery in Alaska was built at Klawock, on Prince of Wales Island in Southeast in 1879. The industry grew very quickly as corporations active in the south looked eagerly at the untapped resource in Alaska. In 1888 seventeen canneries operated in the territory; the next year, thirty-seven canneries packed 714,000 cases. In the early 1890s, overproduction led to consolidation. Alaska Packers Association controlled 80 percent of the pack for most of that decade, packing a million cases a year by 1900. Unlike the Columbia, where Chinook or king salmon was the dominant fish, in Alaska the sockeye or red salmon dominated, though later, in the 1930s, all five major species were packed, including chum or dog salmon. While fishermen initially relied mainly on gill nets, by 1900 many relied heavily on fish traps, sophisticated net systems hanging on piles driven into the sea floor. The piles were arranged so that the fish encountered the net barrier as they attempted to enter a stream mouth. The netting guided them away from the shore and into a heart-shaped container, then into a smaller "spiller," and finally into a "pot," from which they were brailed (lifted by hand nets on long poles) into a scow, which moved them to the onshore factory. The traps were extraordinarily efficient, taking virtually all the fish in a run when they were in operation. Later, innovators perfected floating versions, which could be moved from place to place to intercept more than one run of a species, increasing efficiency still more. Traps were used primarily in Southeast where the fish moved in smaller schools. In western Alaska, along the coast of the Bering Sea, gill nets and seine nets deployed in river bays caught huge concentrations of fish, making traps unnecessary.

A salmon cannery represented a substantial investment. The thirty-seven canneries operating in Alaska in 1889 represented a commitment of $4 million. They employed between five and six thousand people and nearly one hundred steam vessels. Just one cannery plant alone—comprising the canning factory, with its cleaning machines (the "Iron Chinks," mechanical cleaners invented in 1903), the conveyors, cooking pots, soldering room, and cans—cost hundreds of thousands of dollars to construct, operate, and maintain. Then there were the bunkhouses and mess hall, the power plant, infirmary, warehouse, and other outbuildings, together with a dock and lifting facility for loading and unloading, and the boats, gear, and traps for catching fish. In addition, most companies brought at least some, and in many cases, all their workforce from San Francisco or Seattle. Even with contract labor and discounted wages (for medical costs, special clothing, transportation), the cost of the workforce was high. The companies that operated the canneries were incorporated in Washington or California, but the investors came from across the nation.

Though they represented a huge investment in Alaska resource extraction, the salmon packers had a mixed economic impact on the territory. They created few permanent jobs and supported few businesses in the territory. As much as possible, they brought their own supplies with them on the same ship they used to carry the cases of canned salmon back to Seattle and San Francisco at the end of the season. To be sure, there were a number of resident fishermen, small independent operators, who purchased some supplies in the region. And both Native and non-Native fishermen increasingly sold to the canneries as independent contractors. But the economic impact was negligible compared to the mining industry. In the beginning, before the Congress authorized a small tax on production, the greatest impact of the canned salmon industry on the territory was environmental, not economic.

⊱⊰

Most of the eight thousand non-Natives in Alaska in the 1890s had not come to stay. In the canneries along the southeast and Bering Sea coasts they were mostly men who worked seasonally and returned south, mostly to the Pacific Northwest and California, for the winter. Along the interior rivers the prospectors were also mostly men. Many worked seasonally, but an appreciable number worked through the winter, melting the permafrost with surface fires and lifting out the thawed overburden as they dug their way toward ancient river gravels or gold-bearing quartz. But few expected to make their homes in the Yukon basin. Their reason for being in the north was to return rich to the south, though few realized that aspiration.

In Juneau and Sitka, circumstances were somewhat different. The residents in each of these towns devoted considerable energy to community building. Sitka, particularly, took on an appearance of stability and urban refinement. The society of government officials and functionaries, missionary families, and military men and their wives gave a cachet of culture to the place. It boasted a Literary and Dramatic Association, and housed the collection of the Alaskan Society of Natural History and Ethnology, mostly gathered by Sheldon Jackson on his various Alaska travels. A New York journalist wrote in 1893 that Sitka was "the center of gayety and fashion." Not surprisingly, the same reporter thought Juneau richer in business and commerce. The federal payroll supported Sitka while Juneau depended on private sector enterprise. Many men brought wives and families with them, or sent for them after they were sure of their employment or their prospects, but there was less time in Juneau for community building.

But even in Sitka and Juneau most residents were apparently those Richard White has called "modern migrants," those in the territory to make money, which they would then transport back to the contiguous states, back "home." Alaska was a sojourn, an adventure, a temporary opportunity. "Alaska is not a region of homes and householders," David Starr Jordan wrote in 1899. True civic responsibility lay long in the future. The adventurous people attracted to Sitka and Juneau might tolerate their remote isolation for a time, but most did not intend that their grandchildren should grow up in so unconnected a place as Alaska.

And they certainly had not come to Alaska to suffer. Modern migrants expected to better their circumstances, by which they meant primarily their material circumstances. Sitka and Juneau reflected these values well. The settlers—miners and their families and superintending personnel, the tradesmen of the town and their families, missionaries, government officials—put in place as quickly and comprehensively as they could the built environment, community institutions, economic enterprise, and cultural values of late nineteenth-century America. The schools and churches they erected and the businesses they established, and the expectations they had for these, were an imitation of what they had known.

$$\bowtie \bowtie$$

In 1879 the poet-naturalist John Muir journeyed to Alaska where, accompanied by the Presbyterian missionary Samuel Hall Young and guided by a several Stikeen Indians, he paddled by canoe from Wrangell in the southern part of the Alexander Archipelago to Glacier Bay in the north. He reveled in the rugged wilderness he saw. For Muir, nature was God's plan made manifest. All existence, Muir thought, had intrinsic value. Plants, mountains, glaciers, animals, all had their own meaning and did not need a utilitarian context for validation. For Muir, nature was the source of spirituality, a powerful repository of meaning in life. All his encounters with it were positive.

Thus, Muir was particularly disturbed by the commodification of nature in nineteenth-century American culture. American industry and technology in the last half of the century seemed to many to have subdued nature. A cumulating series of inventions and entrepreneurial innovations raised the material standard of living of many Americans, and gave them leisure time and discretionary income. Their relationship with nature was rendered increasingly remote and less tangible by widespread availability of new products. Few understood nature in Muir's terms. "To obtain a hearing on behalf of nature from any other standpoint than that of human use is almost impossible," he wrote. For the overwhelming majority of Americans, the purpose of the land and the species of flora and fauna it supported and the minerals it contained was to enrich human independence, and improve their material environment.

This is certainly how Alaska's new settlers understood nature, as did the absentee investors who brought the Treadwell Mines and the canned salmon industry into existence, and the prospectors and their backers who staked claims and dug in the creeks and valleys of Alaska's interior. For the prospectors, creeks and rocks were commodities that they exploited through unrelenting, backbreaking labor. For the owners, operators, and miners at Treadwell and the other mines at Juneau, the ore they dug, and the trees they used for shoring and for housing, and the water they used for mucking and for processing and cooling, and all other attributes of the local environment were materials to be appropriated for creating and expanding free enterprise and whatever personal freedom might accompany it. For the cannery owners and operators, the salmon that crowded beyond numbering into Alaska's streams and rivers each spring and summer were so much bounty to be harvested.

Most Americans in the nineteenth century did not consider the alterations and pollution of the landscape associated with industrial and economic growth to be unacceptable costs. In fact, many did not consider them costs at all. Progress in the laissez–faire economic context of the time often meant converting natural resources into industrial and consumer products through wholesale despoliation of the landscape and the resources it supported. Alaska's new residents were at one with American culture in their approach toward nature. As Juneau climbed up the side of its mountain backdrop, few gave much thought to the effect on the environment. It wasn't that the effects weren't visible. Traveling in Alaska in the mid-1880s to prepare a guidebook, Eliza Scidmore noted that the chlorination process used at the Treadwell works had killed all the vegetation on the shore of Gastineau Channel a mile above and below the mines. A similar withering of growth occurred on the mainland shore adjacent to the lode mines there. In the interior at

Treadwell Mines, c. 1895. (Courtesy Alaska State Library: Alaska Purchase Centennial Commission Collection)

the Yukon district mining camps, miners utilized the same landscape-moving techniques that had been perfected in California and elsewhere in the West. Where ancient placers lay beneath shallow overburden, they often used open-cut methods, stripping the ground of vegetation and digging away to bedrock. Hydraulic mining employed long flumes built of wood to carry water to the prospect, using gravity to build pressure, then directing the water at the overburden through high-power nozzles which crumbled the land, which could then be washed through sluices. In other situations, miners diverted streams into, or away from, gulches and ancient streambeds, depending on their needs. Some built fires to melt holes in the permafrost, successively cleaning out the holes and refiring in them until they reached the ancient gravels or lodes.

The salmon fishery produced the most destructive environmental impact in the early period of Alaska's development. Even though traps did not come into widespread use until the beginning of the twentieth century, more primitive fishing techniques were equally destructive, until federal legislation prohibited them. The most effective method was barricading streams with log walls built into the stream from bank to bank. The salmon schooled when they encountered the wall, and the brailers used dipnets on long poles to load them into a scow. If the barricade was left in the stream during the entire run, which was often the case, no salmon moved upstream to propagate the species. Widespread use of gillnets at the entrance to streams also could be devastating, since these were often stretched completely across the stream entrance. Again, if the nets were left in place through the entire run, no fish could enter the stream.

There were other pressures on the environment. Virtually everywhere non-Natives congregated, they hunted game to supplement their diets, as well as buying meat from the Natives. At Sitka, the three hundred Army troops and approximately six hundred new settlers placed substantial demand on the available resource. Soon after the founding of Juneau, wild game resources on Douglas Island and in the vicinity of the new town were inundated. Before long Juneauites consumed more imported beef than wild game because the latter became too difficult to find. But in the mining camps particularly, game constituted the major food item. Wherever miners established themselves in appreciable numbers, the game population suffered. Historian Morgan Sherwood concluded that such hunting was a minor threat to game in the nineteenth century because the non-Native population was still small. But the practice was not halted effectively until the foundation of the Alaska Game

Commission in 1925. And the numbers were significant. Five thousand caribou were apparently killed in the Fortymile district in 1894, the year before the major rush there. Far to the south, in an area on the Kenai Peninsula, an outdoor writer counted five hundred sheep in 1897; only a fraction of that number survived just three years later.

Fatalism characterized much thought about wildlife, and about nature, in nineteenth-century America. In 1885 Frederick Schwatka, an Army lieutenant who had climbed Chilkoot Pass and descended the Yukon River, published a trade press account of his observations of the north. Some species would become extinct, Schwatka averred, for example the musk ox, which had once been important in Eskimo life. Though some remained in the eastern Arctic, the last musk ox native to Alaska had been killed in 1865, nearly all taken by Native hunters. The animal was a remnant of a "great race," Schwatka said, "a species that has seen its best days far in the past, and is slowly traveling the road to extinction."

The history of game hunting in Alaska is illustrative of the attitudes of Alaska's new residents toward their environment. Generally, they regarded the game supply as inexhaustible because of Alaska's size and the idea that a wilderness was a place of abundant game. The extinction of the musk ox, an exotic species unfamiliar to most non-Natives, did not suggest to them that other species might also become extinct. Thus, they resented and resisted legislation to protect game, regarding such measures variously as stemming from the ignorance, or misplaced zeal, of eastern elitists interested only in trophies

Salmon canners in early Alaska had a different response to the question of resource exhaustion. In his landmark study of the politics of conservation in the Alaska canned salmon industry, Richard Cooley found that operators recognized early that Alaska's fisheries were in danger of depletion. In 1889 an inspector for the U.S. Fish Commission, appalled at the effect of stream barricades, compared the Alaska fishery to the depleted California and the Columbia River fisheries and predicted that only federal regulation could save Alaska. His and other analysts' dire predictions seemed to convince the owners that regulation was necessary, but they could not agree on how restrictive it should be. And they pinned great hope on developing hatcheries. With artificial propagation, one spokesman assured his fellows, the fishery could never become depleted, for each year more fish would be released than could be caught. Unfortunately, hatcheries did not work, but that did not become apparent until well into the twentieth century. In the meantime, Congress passed a measure acceptable to the industry in 1896. It prohibited fishing above

The Antelope with a bumper catch of salmon. (Courtesy Courtland Smith)

tidewater, where intensive fishing was most destructive, in streams less than five hundred feet wide. In larger rivers, nets, traps, and other gear could be stretched across only one-third of the stream. Further, all gear, wherever placed, had to be one hundred yards apart from any other gear. But the act manifested the industry's confidence in artificial propagation by requiring that every cannery start a hatchery. Ineffective enforcement of all these provisions, however, invited widespread disregard of the act's prohibitions and mandates.

❧ ❧

By the end of the century, then, the beginnings of economic development in Alaska replicated the most fundamental aspects of American character and culture. Development depended in the first instance on the discovery of natural resources which absentee investors were willing to gamble on. The only non–Native American town in the territory floundered after a vigorous start because there was no economic base. Only when a natural resource had been identified that could attract outside capital for its exploitation, creating jobs and a potential local economy, did appreciable numbers return. When they did, they brought with them the essential characteristics of their late nineteenth-century American culture. That culture was materialist and dependent; its citizens demanded federal support, but expected that they should be free of federal restrictions. They were racist, and unconcerned with their impact on their environment. They were motivated primarily by their solid belief in the legitimacy and efficacy of individual economic self-reliance, while paradoxically, at the same time dependent on economic forces they could not control, and which many likely did not understand. More of their brethren would follow these early settlers at the end of the century, and with them Alaska would see more manifestations of American culture. The impact on the territory would be substantial, but not characteristically different. Only the numbers would change.

2

Pioneer Alaskans, Their Environment, and Alaska Natives

⊁ ⊰

Pierre Berton, interpreter of the great Klondike gold rush, said that mad stampede north at the turn of the century was an event like none other in history. In August 1896, a wizened veteran prospector named George Carmacks and his Indian companions, Kate Carmacks and Tagish Charlie, discovered vast placer gold deposits on a Yukon River tributary in Canada bigger than any seen before or since. Once evidence arrived in Seattle and San Francisco of the truth of the fantastic stories about fabulous amounts of placer gold just waiting to be picked off the ground, thousands of argonauts dropped what they were doing, frantically cobbled together an "outfit," and in a fever lit out for Dawson, most of them leaving their families and livelihoods behind. The most intrepid scaled Chilkoot Pass, the trail to which rises from sea level to 3500 feet in 16 miles, including an elevation gain of 2500 feet in the last 4 miles, creating an indelible image of fortitude and tenacity that has become symbolic of the frontier north, rugged determination pitted against a formidable, threatening environment. An estimated forty thousand trekkers went over Chilkoot and White passes and floated down the Yukon to Dawson, most during the winter of 1897-98. There were twenty thousand people in Dawson by the summer of 1898. Predictably, few struck gold. Berton suggests that, at most, four thousand found pay dirt and of those only four hundred in quantities such that one could say they made their fortunes. By 1901 Dawson's population had atrophied to fewer than one thousand.

What almost all of the pioneers sought in the north was the opportunity to build a better life for themselves and their progeny, the same thing their predecessors had sought at Sitka and Juneau. They were as dedicated to the replication of mainstream American culture as those a generation earlier. Even in the towns that were temporary, such as Iditarod, Candle, and Knik, they built according to the only culture they knew, one of economic individualism and free enterprise, with generous support from the federal government. Since so few struck it rich, the towns at first comprised people who had brought enough capital with them to import their goods by river steamer from the coast, or had brought them over the trail. The argonauts' diaries told of all manner of goods and technologies being lugged over Chilkoot Pass, everything from printing presses to barrels of whiskey. The new seekers and settlers quite literally brought their culture with them to the northland.

The Alaska gold rush attracted sustained attention from two main sources: the federal government and potential investors. The U.S. Congress responded to the increased population of non–Natives in Alaska immediately, without waiting to determine its permanence. In 1898 Congress passed a homestead act for the territory, and authorized an agricultural assessment and experiment program. The next year lawmakers authorized the U.S. Army Signal Corps to find a route for and build a telegraph line that could be connected to the contiguous states by undersea cable. In 1900 Congress passed an omnibus civil government act which moved the capital from Sitka to Juneau, where there was a greater concentration of citizens, added two judges, authorized the drafting of a civil and criminal legal code, repealed prohibition, and authorized the incorporation of towns, giving them the power of local taxation. In addition, they provided a system of annual liquor and business licenses so as to create territorial revenue. There were other congressional responses as well, including Alaska's first game law, that prohibited the wanton destruction of wild birds, their nests and eggs. Still more legislation followed within a few years, including an act to provide funding from within the territory for education and road construction. Then in 1906 Congress approved biennial election of a non–voting delegate to the House of Representatives, and a fourth judge for Alaska. And in the same year lawmakers brought an aspect of Indian acculturation policy to the territory with the Alaska Native Allotment Act.

With these responses, Congress treated Alaska as if its new settlers were embarked on planting a traditional American society, one characterized by self-sufficient agriculture, by commercial enterprise, by

Guggenheim critic
James Wickersham.
(Courtesy Anchorage Museum of
History and Art)

the rule of law, and acculturation of the Native population. Though they did not think Alaska yet warranted full territorial status, congressmen and senators nonetheless were quick to adopt measures to nurture settlement through expanded civil power, access to law, and local self-government. In 1908, James Wickersham, who had come to the territory as one of the two judges added in 1900, resigned his judgeship to run for delegate to Congress. Elected, he served six successive terms, from 1908 to 1920. Wickersham went to Washington just as Progressive reform was gathering its greatest strength. In Congress he argued that Alaska residents should not be denied that most basic right of Americans, government by consent of the governed, and persuaded Congress in 1912 to authorize election of a bicameral, biennial territorial legislature. As with other territorial legislatures, Congress could disallow any of its legislation, but that seldom-used provision seemed a minor irritant when measured against the increased control the settlers felt over their affairs and their destiny.

Wickersham utilized Progressive reform sentiment in his election campaigns in Alaska. Having recently come to Alaska from various states where politicians ran increasingly as reform candidates, Alaska voters were familiar with reform issues, and reform rhetoric. Wickersham had a highly visible, ubiquitous foil for his Progressive campaigns in the Guggenheim Corporation, which sought to develop copper deposits in the Wrangell Mountains of south-central Alaska. Development costs were great, and the corporation found a partner in J. Pierpont Morgan, the financier, with whom they formed the Alaska Syndicate. With the combined financing, they were able to complete the Copper River and Northwestern Railway in 1911. The coastal terminus of the line generated a new Alaska town, Cordova. The Syndicate also bought the Alaska Steamship Company for supplying their Alaska operations.

The Guggenheim Corporation had great plans for Alaska. They intended to develop coal deposits in the so-called Bering River field, near the mouth of the Copper River not far from Cordova, to fuel the railroad and the mines, and for the general market in Alaska and elsewhere. The deposits were thought to be very rich, containing untold wealth in "black diamonds." There were oil deposits associated with the coal, also. In addition, they planned to construct a smelter on Prince William Sound to make the copper ingots and thus save the expense of shipping raw ore south. But they had even grander plans. They would extend the railroad inland to the Yukon River, linking steamboat and barge service on the interior rivers with the coast. This would make feasible acquisition and development of additional mining prospects in Alaska's interior. Then they would purchase the steamship line to service their holdings in the territory and ship out such mineral wealth as those holdings might generate. This integrated scheme represented colonial capitalism at its height. All the investment, and nearly all the labor force, would come from outside the territory, and would be completely in the control of the few directors of the investment group. The purchase of the Chitina district copper claims in 1906 was a first step in organizing this potential coordinated blueprint for Alaska development.

Wickersham used the threat of a Guggenheim virtual monopoly on Alaska resource development to galvanize the Alaska electorate, and to pressure Congress for still more federal support. He was hugely successful in Congress as the wave of reform began to crest after the 1914 presidential election. Wickersham shamed the Congress with images of an Alaska "locked up by the corporate giants." Only competition could save the territory, he insisted. But costs in Alaska were so great that no potential competitors could find the financing to construct an alternate route. It was the government's responsibility, then, Wickersham insisted. The federal government would have to step in to save Alaska for America and for Alaskans.

Perhaps remarkably, the federal government did just that. In 1914 Congress authorized survey, construction, and operation of a railroad which became the Alaska Railroad. The president chose the route, up the Susitna River and over Broad Pass to the Tanana River and into Fairbanks. Construction began in 1915 and was virtually complete by 1918. President Warren Harding went to the territory in 1923 to drive the golden spike in the new bridge over the Tanana River at Nenana. The Alaska Railroad is a permanent monument to federal support for Alaska development. The government's role in railroad construction in Alaska exceeded even the massive land grants made for construction of the transcontinental rail lines, for only in Alaska did the government take direct action, building, owning, and operating the railroad itself rather than subsidizing private investors. This subsidy was not an exception in terms of federal support for Alaska, but just the most comprehensive example of such support.

Congress's response to Guggenheim plans for Alaska development complemented the new Progressive Era conservation policy in the territory. In 1906, just as the Syndicate was developing its Alaska plans, President Theodore Roosevelt prohibited the extraction of coal from all lands in the U.S. (including Alaska). Roosevelt and his advisors worried that private corporations were appropriating basic resources that had national strategic significance. This effectively ended the Guggenheim plan for coal development and a copper smelter in Alaska. Denied Alaska coal, the Syndicate would need to import coal from Canada to run the railroad and the copper mines, significantly increasing the cost of both operations. The corporation also scrapped plans for extension of their railroad to the Yukon River. But they did proceed with development of the copper mines and construction of the Copper River and Northwestern Railway. They also purchased the Northwestern Steamship Company, renaming it Alaska Steamship Company, and purchased Northwestern's cannery holdings.

Cordova was virtually a company town in much the same way that Juneau was. Its reason for existence was the copper mines and the railroad that served them. The people who lived and worked there depended solely on the Alaska Syndicate for their livelihoods and futures. They manifested their loyalty with a particularly spectacular gesture in 1911. On May 3, to protest the "lock up" of Alaska coal, a crowd of about three hundred citizens gathered to burn Gifford Pinchot, Chief of the U.S. Forest Service and an ardent conservationist, in effigy. Then they marched resolutely to the Alaska Steamship Company dock on the waterfront, and began to shovel several hundred tons of Canadian coal from the dock where it had been landed into the bay, shouting, "Give Us Alaska Coal!" National newspapers reported the incident with great glee, immediately christening it the "Cordova Coal Party," evocative of the Boston Tea Party. The president of the Chamber of Commerce was among the shovelers. Company officials opposed the affair, though they sympathized with the protestors. Though the demonstration had no effect on U.S. conservation policy, it showed that those Alaskans dependent on absentee investors were as willing to attack the federal government as to accept help from it. The enemy was whoever threatened economic development.

In 1899 Alaska experienced a particularly strange event that highlighted the economic dependence of the territory and the stark contrast between the powerful who determined Alaska's destiny from afar and the powerless whose futures they controlled. Edward H. Harriman, the railroad magnate, gathered together more than a score of scientists from museums, government agencies, and universities for a trip to Alaska on an elegant steamship he leased for the purpose, the *George W Elder*. Harriman's personal objective was to kill an Alaska brown bear on Kodiak Island. He may also have been investigating the possibility of a railroad connection between Asia and America across the Bering Strait. The ship sailed from Seattle with an astonishing coterie which included the scientists, Harriman and his family—wife, two daughters, and two sons— and servants, stenographers, a physician and assistant, a nurse, a chaplain, eleven hunters, and various packers and camp hands. The crew included sixty-five officers and men. The ship carried all the necessities of travel, and indeed, life, and a great many amenities. The manifest included motor launches and canoes, weapons, horses, tents, a piano and an organ, a library, the latest audio equipment, steers, sheep, turkeys, chickens, and a milk cow for food, and cases of champagne and thin-stemmed glasses from which to drink it. It was opulence afloat, designed to be utterly independent of the world it should sail through, self-reliant and aloof. Harriman and his scientists set out to see Alaska, but only on their own terms, not nature's. John Muir, who had twenty years earlier explored coastal Alaska in a small canoe, must have been exceedingly uncomfortable on this journey. He had already written of his despair at "arm chair tourists" who booked passage on the railroad company steamers that sailed north from Seattle up the famous "inland passage," skirting some of the most thrilling scenery in the world, but seldom engaging it directly or personally. When these passengers did get off the ship, it was usually just to take photographs with their new Kodak box cameras, thoughtlessly strewing the protective film papers around the landscape. The Harriman party probably did not litter, but otherwise there was little to separate them from the hordes of wealthy cruise passengers

Sailing up the coast, Harriman's luxury liner meandered in and out of the canals, bays, and coves of the serpentine coastline, stopping nightly, and often during the day. The scientists gave lectures, and gathered flora and fauna at the various stops. After the novelty of the cruise had worn off, the passengers took turns presenting entertainments, and someone devised a cheer for them all: "Who are we? Who are we? We are, We are H.A.E.," the Harriman Alaska Expedition.

Harriman shot his bear on Kodiak Island, but only after his beaters spent three days looking for it. Continuing on, they sailed north across the Bering Sea. When the ship sailed into the Bering Strait, the expedition was mere miles from the throngs of argonauts, hopefuls, laborers, dancehall girls, and hangers-on crowded on the Nome beach, hoping to strike it rich and join the likes of Harriman and his compeers in the rare world of luxury and power, but with little realistic likelihood of doing so. In the Bering Strait the *George W. Elder* passed also among several whaling ships, whose crews were engaged in the dangerous business of killing the huge mammals from small whaleboats. But the Harriman expedition took no interest in the gold rush and little in the whalers. They were removed, apart, aloof, symbolically at least, and for all intent and purpose, in actuality.

The Harriman expedition did help to highlight growing national concern about the future of Alaska's natural resources, however, by publication of fourteen volumes of photos, drawings, and articles about the expedition by the participants. That concern would grow rapidly during the Progressive Era, resulting in significant new protection for wildlife habitat, and for strategic resources. Federal conservation measures taken soon after the turn of the century would save both animal species and resource deposits from wholesale exploitation by frontier settlers and corporate investors.

When the *George W. Elder* cruised Prince William Sound, the passengers delighted in the magnificent splendor of its extraordinary wilderness and in the appearance of many species of flora and fauna, including puffins, various kinds of seals, killer whales, eagles, marbled murrelets, and many others. They even discovered an unknown fiord, into which they daringly took the vessel over an ice bar and between glacial walls; they named it Harriman Fiord. But one species they did not see in the region was the sea otter, for it had been hunted out first by the Russians, and then, after 1867, the American prospector/trappers. The otters would be absent from Sound until, under protection, they were brought back to this natural habitat by the U.S. Fish and Wildlife Service in the 1950s. Today, there are nearly fifteen thousand sea otters in Prince William Sound, despite the tragedy of the *Exxon Valdez*. By the same token, where it took three days for Harriman's beaters to scare up a bear for him to shoot on Kodiak Island, and an old sow with cubs at that, today it is probably not possible to go three hours out of Kodiak City without seeing a bear, perhaps not three miles. This, too, is a triumph of federal conservation policy, the bears on Kodiak Island having been under federal protection since the beginning of the twentieth century.

The distance the members of the Harriman Alaska Expedition placed between themselves and the common herd on the Nome beach and the common sailors of the Arctic whaling fleet when they sailed through Bering Strait suggests a deep social alienation, a failure to recognize and connect with vital human elements in their surroundings. But they were not the only ones with myopia. The argonauts and whalers themselves also chose alienation as a mode of existence; in their case, it was distance and estrangement from the Native population and from the environment itself. The impact of the new, larger population of non-Natives on both was substantial. First, and perhaps foremost, Natives lost control over areas where they traditionally had lived and used resources. In the first instance this was because they were attracted to the white communities where they found useful technologies and beguiling amenities. At the same time, increasing numbers of whites brought pressure on existing Native areas as they tramped the ground searching for signs of gold. And the whites competed with the Natives for the land's bounty. Historian Morgan Sherwood wrote that "each miner brought a gun, an outdoorsman's appetite, and perhaps a hungry sled dog. . . Many did their own hunting. Others relied on white or Native market hunters." As noted in chapter 1, native hunters seeking to profit from the sale of meat to the whites killed many animals. Sherwood wrote that the slaughter was reminiscent of the buffalo hunt on the Great Plains in the 1870s, only this time the Natives did most of the killing.

Government agents, assisted by knowledgeable and sympathetic visitors interested in species survival, collected data and anecdotes. Members of the prestigious national Boone and Crockett Club, for example, told of the wanton slaughter of game by Natives, white residents, and "so-called sportsmen" throughout the territory. Arguing for a stronger game law, Madison Grant, a mammalogist and member of Boone and Crockett, presented an argument, which was anathema to Alaskans. The fish and game resources of Alaska did not belong alone to the Native and non-Native residents of the territory, he said; they did not have any inherent right to them. Instead, they belonged to all Americans, in whose interest, he thought, they should be protected. "In Alaska," Sherwood quoted him as saying, "we have our last chance to preserve and protect rather than to restore." This concept of public ownership of resources on the public domain was the essence of Progressive Era conservation policy, though the management regime stressed efficient or so-called "wise use," not preservation.

But this did little to stop the carnage, for most of the governors accepted the twin convictions of resident Alaskans regarding the plentifulness of game and their right to it. So violations continued unabated. Restaurants and hotels in Anchorage, for example, routinely served moose meat out of season, identifying it on their menus as "top sirloin steak hunter style," or "stew hunter style."

What is significant about these stories is the attitude regarding Alaska and its resources that they show. Alaska's residents were not malicious; they thought they were doing what pioneers in America always had done, and perhaps they were. But experience demonstrated that such attitudes quickly led to the destruction of game supplies, and often enough threatened species. In the same way that they were fatalistic about the extinction of Natives in America, so were nineteenth-century Americans fatalistic about the disappearance of the once ubiquitous passenger pigeon, and of course, the buffalo.

The slaughter of the whales in the Bering Sea and the Arctic Ocean at the same time that non-Natives were flooding into the territory at the turn of the century had a significant impact on coastal Native communities. Normally the whalers brought enough supplies to satisfy their needs through the season. But if the crews were marooned in the Arctic, they often relied on meat supplied by Native hunters. It was not unusual for groups of villagers to move close to the whaling camps and to provide caribou and other meat for as long as a year. A number of studies have assessed the nature of the impact on the Native people, noting that when the Natives were hunting for the whalers, they were not hunting for themselves or preserving meat for their own needs.

The number of whales taken was enormous. John R. Bockstoce and Daniel B. Botkin calculated that between 1849 when whalers first entered the Arctic and 1914 when exploitation there ended, whalers killed well over eighteen thousand bowhead whales. Nearly all of these were caught and processed into whale oil and the various industrial uses of whalebone. The industry collapsed soon after the turn of the twentieth century because there were too few bowheads left to pay the costs of the hunting voyages.

The whalers were only visitors on the Bering and the Arctic, interested in the profit they could bring home. Like the managers of the salmon canneries, like the dilettantish Harriman party, they brought most of what they needed with them, and except for emergencies, which were, unfortunately, all too frequent, they were self-reliant. More pertinent for this study is their attitude toward Alaska's resources. Like the argonauts, like the investors in the canned salmon industry, like the Morgan-Guggenheim Alaska Syndicate, the whalers regarded the resources they preyed on as theirs to appropriate, theirs to commodify. That those resources might become extinct did not seem to affect them at all.

Some whalers did acknowledge their responsibility for the over-harvesting of walrus, which began in the 1870s. Whalers turned to walrus each spring when the bowhead whales had migrated past them on their way to the Beaufort Sea. Walrus yielded much less oil and blubber for nearly the same work as a bowhead. But the whalers took them nonetheless, rather than remain idle through the summer while waiting for the bowheads' return migration. The number of walrus slaughtered far surpassed the number of whales. Bockstoce and Botkin estimate one hundred fifty thousand, which is astounding, particularly considering that the total population when the killing began was only about two hundred thousand. No game population could stand that level of harvest, and the whale men soon came to the conclusion that the walrus would disappear. Bockstoce quotes Captain Ebenezer Nye, writing to a New Bedford newspaper in 1879. "Another year or perhaps two years will finish them, - there will hardly be one left, and I advise all Natural History societies and museums to get a specimen while they can. I see no help for them if the whale men continue to take them as they have in past years; they, like the dodo, will become extinct."

Though in the early 1850s as many as two hundred vessels worked the area north and west of Bering Strait, in the 1870s, the years of greatest carnage of the walrus herds, the number fell from fifty-eight to thirty-one, reaching a low for the decade in 1874 with just nineteen vessels in the region. But even nineteen vessels could wreck havoc on the herds, and did. Scores and even hundreds of the large, bulky animals could be taken in a single hunt. Though the walrus were easily frightened, if the sailors placed the first several shots well, killing rather than wounding the animals, which lay in mounds on floating pans of ice, so that the afflicted raised no alarm, firing could continue until the guns were too hot to hold. In such circumstances the walrus had no chance, and with them, those Natives who depended on them nearly exclusively for food.

The walrus slaughter was disastrous for the coastal Native population. The eradication of the animals nearly resulted in the eradication of the Inuit villages on the Diomedes, and on St. Lawrence and King islands. The same year that Captain Nye waxed nostalgic for the walrus herds, Natives died in great numbers because of his and his colleagues' slaughter. Whalers reported to the U.S. Revenue Cutter *Rush* that year that in three villages on St. Lawrence Island all the people had died for lack of food. Nye himself reported in the same letter that a third of the population below St. Lawrence had perished. Many Natives had come on board the whale ships begging for whatever food they might get to feed their families. In 1880 when the fleet arrived at St. Lawrence Island the whalers found Natives wrapped in blankets lying on sleeping platforms, dead from starvation. Bodies were found stacked one on the other in their small houses. One man was found dead stretched out behind the sled in which he had been pushing a dead companion. One Native family starved for every one hundred walrus taken, Captain Bernard Cogan calculated. Some whale men responded by bringing supplies north for the starving Natives, but such remedies, however humane, could only be partial and temporary. Only restoration of the walrus population through protection would save the Natives of these villages.

Some of the whaling captains acknowledged their contribution to the tragedy and vowed to take no more walrus. But others attempted to avert responsibility by blaming other factors. Alcohol debilitated the Native hunters, some claimed, desensitizing them to their responsibilities and the needs of their families. Bockstoce suggests that even the large amounts of alcohol that became available in the villages with the advent of the whaling fleet likely would not have so incapacitated the hunters as to lead to starvation; this is a reasonable speculation, but it is beside the point, since it was the whalers who brought the alcohol. To survive, the Native people had to accommodate to the changed circumstances brought to their world by the invasive whaling fleet.

In its regulation of the Pacific and western Arctic whale fisheries, the federal government did nothing to preserve the whales, and little to save the walrus, directing its attention only to controlling smuggling, and to protecting the Natives from exploitation. It took a different approach to the canned salmon industry, though its efforts were generally paltry and ineffective. The Pacific canned salmon industry became the great symbol of exploitation of natural resources in Alaska. Despite the congressional law protecting stream mouths above tidewater, passed, as we have seen, in 1896, despoliation of the fishery continued, due to inadequate enforcement of the law and the willingness of operators to violate it. Indeed, violation of fishery regulations was endemic and recognized as such by federal enforcement officials. In 1908 one inspector found on a three-day, three-hundred-mile trip in southeast Alaska twenty-nine trap operators "brazenly violating the law," four engaged in minor or technical violations, and only one confining strictly to the regulations.

When in 1912 it provided Alaska with a territorial legislature, Congress pointedly left control of the fishery in federal hands, though all other territories had gained control of fisheries regulation in their territorial enabling acts. But no territory or state had a fishery like Alaska's. Its geographical limits are difficult to convey. It extends two thousand miles along Alaska's south coast from the southeast panhandle to the Bering Sea. But the straight-line distances are misleading, for the coast is uneven and indented with bays and estuaries. All of Southeast is made up of an archipelago of over a thousand islands, many of them large, and all with bays, inlets, and coves, nearly all of which contribute to the fishery. Salmon are taken throughout the archipelago, and to the westward in Yakutat Bay, Prince William Sound, Cook Inlet, around Kodiak Island, along the Alaska Peninsula, and in Bristol Bay, the latter the world's most prolific salmon fishery. Taken together, this is a truly vast fishery. It produces more salmon than anywhere else and they have long been recognized as a national treasure.

The canned salmon industry lobbied hard against territorial jurisdiction over the fishery because mechanisms for influencing federal regulators were already well in place, and the industry judged, surely correctly, that territorial jurisdiction would mean more regulation and more taxes on what they considered their own fishery. This attitude bred a deep and long-standing resentment in Alaska, leading virtually all of the territory's major politicians into opposition to the industry, Alaskans' resentment of the federal government degenerated to contempt when it became clear that the Congress would not appropriate sufficient funds for adequate enforcement of federal fishery regulations.

The Alaska Packers' Association, the principal industry combine, supported an aggressive lobby in Washington, D.C. In periods of abundance the industry was easily able to persuade Congress to allow the Bureau of Fisheries to relax the regulations in the name of greater efficiency. This inevitably led to depletion of the resource, which led the industry to plead for still more relaxation. Few in Congress, or in Washington, D.C., for that matter, where the Bureau of Fisheries policy judgments were made, had much experiential appreciation of the conditions of the Alaska fishery, and thus were at the mercy of whatever representation industry spokesmen might make. Although Congress established a policy of 50 percent escapement from the fishery in the White Act of 1924, successive legislatures never appropriated sufficient funds to guarantee effective enforcement. This led Alaska's delegate to Congress, Dan Sutherland, an unreconstructed anti-monopoly Progressive, to charge on the floor of the House of Representatives that the failure to pay for enforcement constituted government collusion with the canning industry against the Alaska resource and its fishermen.

The role of frontier Alaskans in the salmon fishery is instructive. They supported restrictions on the industry, but not enough to drive the canneries out of business. By the 1920s, a significant number of Alaskans made their living selling fish to the canneries. Not only did Alaskans acquire gear and take fish on their own, but fish piracy and poaching became common. Piracy is stealing fish from fish traps, a relatively easy enterprise since most operators employed only a single guard. Poaching is fishing illegally during a closed period. In their 1969 study of the industry, James A. Crutchfield and Giulio Pontecorvo asserted that 10 percent of the catch in the fishery before modern times came from piracy and poaching. Though canners knew the circumstances fully well, they purchased pirated and poached fish anyway so as to capture as much of the resource for the market as possible.

The Alaskans were not interested in conserving the Alaska fishery, except as an inchoate notion that they didn't want it to disappear. They wanted equal access to it, and if possible, more than equal access. Ernest Gruening in his 1954 polemical history of the territory, *State of Alaska,* capitalized on the symbolic role played by the Alaska canned salmon industry in the territory, as the villain, along with the federal government, of Alaska's persecution. Alaskans held tenaciously to the conviction that forces outside the territory were responsible for the lack of economic development. They were convinced that collusion between the canned salmon industry and the federal government was an evil conspiracy designed to rob them of their right to control their own affairs, stifle the economic development of the territory, and destroy their futures. And the fish trap, identified now as the instrument not only of the destruction of the fishery but also of absentee, corporate control, became the symbol of Alaskans' subjugation. Abolition of fish traps thus became the rallying cry for redress of Alaskan grievances, for Alaskan freedom.

Alaskans believed that economic development would provide them with better lives, would give them greater freedom, would improve their futures. They believed equally strongly that both absentee investors in the territory and the federal government impeded Alaska's economic development. The investors, they believed, pursued development only when and how it suited their own growth and profit generation, not when and how it might contribute to Alaska's general economic and broader improvement. That is why the working people in Alaska, in the mines and in the towns, supported James Wickersham in his persistent anti-monopoly, anti-Guggenheim political campaigns.

At the same time, the new Alaska residents believed that the federal government sought to keep Alaska undeveloped both in the name of resource conservation, and as a cost-saving measure. That was the rationale for the Cordova Coal Party in 1911. If Alaska had more control over the development of its resources, the new residents believed, its citizens could better orchestrate the territory's development, most particularly its independence. The control the Alaskans wanted was for the purpose of commodification; to them resources and land meant money, which translated into the replicated culture they all sought to establish and enjoy in Alaska. Few Alaskans at the time thought in terms of preservation of a last wilderness; they thought, rather, in terms of a last frontier where the resources, they believed, were supposed to be available for their appropriation. They would prosper by converting those resources into personal profit.

In these beliefs Alaskans were at once partially correct and stunningly naive. Certainly, absentee investors and their managers placed the profits of their Alaska investments and the health of their corporations ahead of the interests of Alaskans. They were capitalists; profit was their first, though not their exclusive, responsibility. As the Treadwell Mine development at Juneau made starkly clear, when it was no longer in the corporation's interest to stay and provide jobs, it left the territory. When the Treadwell Mines flooded in 1917, the corporation closed the works for good, deciding that the cost of pumping out and restoring the complex would overwhelm the profit that could be gained by continued operations. This was the same decision made by the Alaska Syndicate in 1938 when they closed the Kennecott Mines, took up their railroad, and left the territory, responding to the depressed price of copper.

On the other hand, Alaskans were wrong in their belief that the federal government was anti-development in Alaska. As the response to the Klondike gold rush illustrates, and as subsequent chapters will confirm, the federal government was swift, comprehensive, and steadfast in its nurturing of non-Native settlement and economic development in Alaska. The Alaska Railroad is representative of the federal government's commitment to developing Alaska. Moreover, Congress would end the anomaly of territorial government in 1958 with the granting of statehood. But as a representative of the interests of the American people, as those are expressed in political action, Congress maintained its conservation interest in the territory throughout the twentieth century. That interest would become paramount with the rise of national environmental consciousness.

But the Alaskans were naive in thinking that increased self-governance would give them independence from either absentee investors or the federal government. Neither control over territorial fisheries or land policy, nor even the full sovereignty of statehood, would change the market forces that drove corporate decisions or the will of the American people expressed through their Congress. These were difficult lessons which would be obscured from Alaskans' perceptions by their convictions of uniqueness, by their remoteness from the mainstream culture they so comprehensively and slavishly sought to replicate, by their habits of opposition, and by their perception of Alaska as a "frontier." We shall examine those lessons in subsequent chapters.

※ ※

Many of the Alaskans who endorsed economic development and greater control over their destiny were Alaska Natives. But with a few exceptions, the Natives of Alaska were nearly as commodified by the territory's new non-Natives as were the whales and walrus the sailors sought, the gold and copper mined by prospectors and corporations, and the salmon that swam into the region's rivers and streams each summer. If the Natives were convenient, they were used; if not, they were treated as expendable, and regularly threatened and subordinated. The white population discriminated against Natives as a matter of course, reflecting the racist attitudes of early twentieth-century American culture elsewhere. On the Chilkoot Trail Natives were packers. At Dawson and Nome, in Fairbanks, Anchorage, and Valdez and around the mining camps they were hunters, suppliers of game, and occasional labor. On the Yukon River they supplied cordwood for the stern-wheelers on the river, and at St. Michael they were stevedores, moving goods off the ocean steamers to the docks and warehouses. The federal schools in Alaska had been segregated from their beginning in 1885 and continued to be so, though Natives would challenge that policy in 1929. Natives lived in all of the white towns, though with few exceptions they were relegated to defined areas of residence, less by the explicit direction of the whites than by habit.

The status of Alaska Natives was different from Indians in the contiguous states and territories because there were no treaties with Alaska Natives. Nor were there formally recognized tribes, for Congress did not have sufficiently detailed ethnographic knowledge on the basis of which to designate tribes. And without tribes and treaties, there were no reservations in Alaska. The question of aboriginal title to the land, then, was effectively postponed to an uncertain time in the future. As the white towns were established, the government simply appropriated the land.

Some Natives adapted quite quickly, and in so doing, retained, or even established, homes in the white towns. Without a formal process such as that mandated by the Dawes Act in the contiguous states to clearly differentiate between acculturated and non-acculturated Natives, those who acted acculturated were often accepted as acculturated.

In 1912, Tlingit and Haida Indians in southeast Alaska formed the first effective regional Native organization in Alaska, the Alaska Native Brotherhood, and an auxiliary, the Alaska Native Sisterhood, in 1915. The general purpose of both groups was to educate and acculturate Alaska Natives. Members had to speak English, sign a sobriety pledge, and accept a mission of service. Both were formed under the aegis of the district superintendent of the Bureau of Education (the federal agency with jurisdiction over services for Alaska Natives) by Christian Natives who had been educated at the Sitka (Presbyterian) Industrial Training School (later the Sheldon Jackson School).

Beginning in 1918, the Tlingit brothers Louis and William Paul took over leadership of the ANB. Both were graduates of Gen. Richard Pratt's Carlisle Indian School in Pennsylvania. William Paul, the younger of the two, would emerge as the more effective leader and would lead the ANB for nearly two decades through strong, intelligent, aggressive leadership. For the Pauls, the question of acculturation was secondary to advocacy of Native rights and Native legitimacy. Indians (and by extension, all Alaska Natives) should pursue Indian interests under Indian leadership, they argued. In the meantime, the ANB would lead in insuring that Indians fulfilled their civic duties as citizens—the Pauls were persuaded that Indians were already citizens by virtue of the 14th Amendment guaranteeing citizenship to all persons born in the U.S.

The Pauls politicized the ANB, and one of their first political targets was the fish trap. Soon after they were elected to leadership positions in the ANB, they adopted abolition of the fish trap as a unifying motif for the organization and for pursuit of Alaska Native interests. The fish trap was as powerful a symbol of oppression for Alaska Natives as it was for non-Natives, in some ways even more, for Alaska Natives, especially near the coast, relied on the salmon fishery.

In 1921 the ANB collected funds to send William Paul to Washington, D.C., to testify against fish traps. Paul told the committee he was an advocate for all the resident fishermen of Alaska, but he focused most of his arguments on the impact of the projected law on Indians. The ANB, he said, represented five thousand Indians; for the last two years these Indians had been facing starvation because of the depletion caused by the industry's over fishing. He told the Congress that Indians soon would not be able

> to buy just the barest necessities of living—sufficient clothing for themselves to cover their bodies; sufficient food of a sufficient variety to place on their tables for their growing children, and sending their children to school.

Paul explained that Indians relied on the fishery in several ways. First, they fished for subsistence. Many families still dried thousands of fish each summer, fishing all the summer months from May to October as the five different salmon species returned at different times. Second, the Indians caught larger amounts of fish, usually with set nets along the beach or at stream mouths, or with seine nets set from fishing boats, which they sold to the various canneries. Third, a number of canneries

William Paul, Tlingit leader.
(Courtesy Frances
DeGermane Paul)

hired native women to work as fish cleaners on the "line," and the women's families often became dependent upon the cash income they earned.

Paul's appearance before Congress was a remarkable occurrence, the first by an Alaska Native as an advocate for a particular policy or program. From the standpoint of the ANB and Indians in Alaska, it was a highly significant event, for one of them was making the Indians' own case, rather than a white man making it for them. William Paul was living proof that Alaska Indians could master the white people's laws and rhetoric, and confront them on their own grounds, playing by their own rules. In this context, whether or not he got results was less significant than the fact that he was there at all.

Many whites applauded Paul's achievement and his advocacy. But some did not. Some canneries did not hire Natives because they found them unreliable. In their position as officers of the ANB, the Paul brothers wrote to those canneries urging them to change their policy, and at their urging the territorial governor, Thomas Riggs, also wrote to several canneries to ask them to hire more Natives. At least one operator responded with an attack on the Pauls. The manager of the Hoonah

Packing Company complained about "squaw men" agitators who prompted villagers to protest hiring practices. "No greater good" could be extended to Alaska Natives, he wrote the governor, "than to dispose of that element . . . and other elements that are extracting some sums of money from them for their ill advice and seeds of propaganda." It is impossible to determine whether the manager's remarks were intended to be political. William Paul made enemies easily. His tactics were often aggressive, his manner confrontational, and his actions often political. Such a combination invited opposition.

Over the next several years the brothers built up the ANB through establishment of new local chapters. In 1922, William Paul organized many villagers into a reliable voting bloc by supplying them with templates to place over their ballots in the voting booth in order to vote for the candidates he endorsed. In 1924 he used this political power base to run successfully for a seat in the territorial legislature.

Predictably, Paul's political success generated substantial opposition. Rival politicians were alarmed at the arrival of a new contender for power and position. Some found bloc voting of illiterate Indians offensive; it seemed to them to violate the American notion of free democracy. Such criticism revealed a latent racism, for a majority of votes in America before the twentieth century were probably cast by illiterates, since universal, compulsory education did not become a feature of American culture until after the Civil War, and the secret vote was not required in national elections until 1892. In fact, much anti–Paul political opposition was clearly racist in character, though perhaps not fully recognized as such by his opponents.

In 1923, the Alaska Legislature, meeting after Paul's success in the 1922 election, took up a voters' literacy bill. The debate was unabashedly racist. One representative, a Juneau businessman who had won his seat despite the opposition of "Paul's Indians," argued that, as a class, the Indians of Alaska constituted "practically all the illiterate voting population of the Territory." It was reprehensible, he said, that manipulators held a balance of power in the electorate and could use the votes of trusting Indians not for the Indians' good, but to support the manipulator's own ambitions. "The Indians, having no vague knowledge of our institutions and government," he said, "lend themselves to the machinations of political charlatans." After hearings and spirited floor debate, the House passed the measure, but it failed in the Senate.

The issue of Indian voting dominated the next election campaign. In the spring primaries all the major candidates took public positions on the issue, and much of the rhetoric was sharply negative. "A small but well organized political ring," the *Alaska Daily Empire* informed its readers, was prepared "to continue the practice of mass voting of illiterate Indians":

> *If the Indians who cannot read and write and who have no conception of the responsibilities of citizenship are to be voted like sheep by a few politicians, the consequences cannot but be disastrous to the Indians themselves. The welfare of the Indians of Southeastern Alaska depend in large measure upon their retaining the friendship of the white people. They have it yet, but the performances in the primaries and the election two years ago strained the feeling almost to the breaking point. The Indians cannot afford to jeopardize their position by permitting designing and office-seeking politicians to lead them into controversial politics.*

The Alaska press reported on debate in the U.S. Congress on an Indian citizenship act for any and all Native Americans. If Indians were made citizens, all Indians would henceforth be potential voters, the *Empire* noted. A territorial literacy act, however, would prevent those who were illiterate from voting for Paul or the candidates or issues he endorsed.

For his part, Paul attempted to broaden his platform to include issues shared by Indians and whites alike, particularly opposition to creation of federal fish reserves and support for higher taxes on the fishing industry. But an avalanche of vehemence on the issue of Indian voting buried anything Paul might say. "A plan is afoot," read a large political ad in the *Empire,* "to extend to the Indians of Alaska all the privileges of whites, including the right to sit on juries, to vote irrespective of mental qualifications, and to send their children to the white schools to mingle, regardless of physical condition, with white children." Unless those opposed "to having Indians in the Legislatures" were to organize, "the Indians are certain to have the balance of power." Three legislators placed a joint ad in which they asserted that they did not seek office for personal reasons, but only "to avert what we believe to be a real danger; for if illiterate Indians control nominations and election of candidates for the legislature, serious trouble is bound to result to all, both whites and Indians." And on the eve of the election, the *Empire* called upon voters not to "cheapen American citizenship." Alaska could not afford "to risk domination in governmental and school affairs by the votes of tribesmen."

Perhaps such overtly racist appeals were too much for many voters, for the primary election results were a complete triumph for William

Paul and the ANB. Paul outpolled all but one candidate in a field of thirteen. Nonetheless, the results exacerbated the campaign rhetoric for the general election. In October the *Empire* asserted that

> *If racial feeling should develop between whites and Indians in Alaska, the responsibility for it will lie with those who are giving the Indians either vicious or foolish advice . . . If those who are trying to rush the Indians to the polls in masses, literate and illiterate, to vote in a bloc, as Indians, have their way they will create a chasm between the races in Alaska that will . . . make this either a white man's country or an Indians' country for many years to come.*

Apparently the editor of the paper could not imagine a climate in which whites and Indians functioned as equal partners, "literate or illiterate." In the campaign, territorial delegate Dan Sutherland supported Paul, and opposed the literacy law, which everyone expected to be a major issue in the 1925 legislature. His endorsement of Paul was a major political gamble.

In actuality, the literacy law was a stand-in for William Paul—racist though the culture was, the electorate could not have tolerated a direct attack on Paul's Indianness, or on Indians directly. One opponent ran large ads in the *Empire* with the headline "Keep Alaska and Its Schools Free From Indian Control." Without a literacy law, his ad read, "the Government of the Territory of Alaska, its institutions, its schools, the government of some of its towns, their institutions and the public schools, will inevitably pass into the hands of those controlling the votes of thousands of illiterates." The *Empire* attacked William Paul not just for his organization of the Indian vote, but also for his opposition to fish traps and his advocacy of additional taxes on the canneries, both ANB positions. New taxes for the fishing industry would be "ruinous," the paper argued, and would bring widespread unemployment and depopulation, as the canneries would not be able to operate at a profit." But the paper still considered the literacy question to be the "main issue before voters."

But in the general election in November 1924 voters again rejected the appeal of those who castigated William Paul and Dan Sutherland. Sutherland won handily, and Paul received the third-highest vote total among House candidates in the division. He would go on to serve two terms in the territorial House. No other Native would be elected to office in Alaska until 1944. It was an extraordinary achievement, particularly given the nature of the campaign that had been waged against him. It was made possible certainly by Paul's association with Sutherland and former Delegate James Wickersham, the mentor of both. Paul was now more than ever a hero among his own people, and the power of the ANB in Alaskan affairs was convincingly demonstrated.

But the challenge to Indian legitimacy was not over. With Paul's victory, the die was cast; now the question of a literacy act would be fought out again in the legislature. As the *Empire* essayed as the final results came, "The Fight Has Just Begun." When the territorial legislature opened in March 1925, the *Empire* reminded legislators that nearly all newspapers in the territory favored the law. Governor Scott Bone, a Harding appointee, urged passage. Endorsements cascaded on Juneau from civic groups throughout Alaska. Commercial clubs and chambers of commerce, women's clubs, the American Legion, and virtually every parent-teachers' association in southeast Alaska were anxious, it seemed, to condemn Indian voting.

Quick action on the measure precluded much of the emotional commentary that had characterized earlier debate. The proposed bill established a literacy qualification, but it protected the franchise for any who had voted previously, including Indians. Although those who had voted for him previously would be "grandfathered" into the law as voters, Paul introduced the ANB's resolution against the literacy bill, and reminded legislators that literacy had not been a requirement in most elections ever held in the United States. His Republican colleagues pointed out that any act that disfranchised previous voters likely would be declared invalid.

The *Empire* fairly fumed. If the "grandfathered" bill were to pass, "it would leave Southeast Alaska little, if any, better off than it is at the present time." It would not bar a single one of the thousand or more "illiterate Indians who have been led to the ballot boxes and voted as a bloc at the dictation of a master." Another deluge of protesting telegrams flooded into Juneau. Lester Henderson, commissioner of the territorial white schools, wrote that the issue was not a matter of politics, but of "territorial welfare." Because of the volatility of the issue, debate was perfunctory, and, following a test vote on an amendment to strike the "grandfather" clause, the bill as written passed unanimously. In an editorial titled "A White Man's Party is Necessary," published one day after the vote, the *Empire* made the racist nature of the debate explicit. The editor wrote that the race problem was the "paramount political issue" in southeastern Alaska. Opposition to Indians, especially in leadership roles, would continue to be an issue in Alaska in the 1930s and the 1940s and even after World War II. Many non-Native Alaskans easily adopted the racism and oppositional character of Alaska politics. Indeed, if anything, anti-Indian sentiment would become even stronger as the stakes increased, first during the Great Depression when the issue was the economic empowerment of Indians, and then during and after World War II when the issue became Indian title to land.

👀 👀

The culture the new non-Native population established in Alaska in the gold rush era had all the marks of the earlier culture established in Sitka, Juneau, and Wrangell. Though many intended to be permanent residents, most still were probably more interested in bettering their economic circumstances in the short term, before returning to the contiguous states. Territorial newspapers regularly carried notices of people retiring "Outside," and while there are no statistics on this issue before the modern period, other aspects of the society are consistent with territorial transiency. Certainly the habit of opposition to the federal government was already well established, the governors, Wickersham and Sutherland as delegates, and the territorial legislature regularly excoriating the Congress, the executive branch, and especially the various federal agencies working in the territory.

The culture of opposition was well established in Alaska in the gold rush era and into the 1920s. So, too, was the culture of greed, although less prevalently than at any other time in Alaska's modern history. Alaska was seen as a land of adventure during the 1920s and 1930s, a land for rugged pioneering. But mining was still touted as the respectable "get rich quick" scheme it always had been. El Dorado was in the north, and riches and the independence they would bring were to be had there for the looking. In analyzing Alaska's colonial history further, we shall ask how the Depression, World War II and the campaign for statehood affected Alaska's colonial culture.

3

At Any Cost:
Pioneer Alaska and Economic Development

ৼ ৼ

For Alaska's non-Native pioneers, the territory in the 1930s and 1940s was the "last frontier." Their notion of settlement was to construct a new society as much like the old mainland America as possible. They had not come to Alaska to subsist; they had come to prosper. Thus, they grasped at any opportunity for economic development. The Great Depression, when its true proportions became known, shook them deeply. Gold production had peaked in 1906, and the rich veins of copper ore in the Kennecott Mines had played out by 1922. The Alaska Syndicate kept the mines open, processing lower grade ore, until the Depression drove the price so low that continued development was unprofitable. Through the 1920s the canned salmon industry provided territorial tax revenue and modest employment opportunities. But federal spending supported many more, through operation of the Alaska Railroad and the growth of the "federal brigade" in such offices as the Bureau of Indian Affairs, the National Park Service, and the Bureau of Fisheries. When the full effects of the Depression struck Alaska, federal expenditures spelled the difference between staying and leaving for many.

During World War II, federal payrolls and contracts surpassed anything Alaskans had ever dreamed of. Everyone had work, money, and new prospects. After the war, federal spending continued, due to Alaska's strategic position in the Cold War. But Alaskan leaders looked for private sources of economic growth, and hoped they had found one when the

U.S. Forest Service lobbied to open the Tongass National Forest to pulp development. Alaskans were willing to overlook the impact of that and other development on Natives and on the environment. The leadership also recognized that statehood, which seemed possible after the war, would depend on development. In their determination to seize any economic opportunity, pioneer Alaskans continued to manifest the values of the culture they worked so assiduously to replicate on the frontier: individualism and the advance of consumerism. They considered all other developmental considerations ancillary.

⊱⊰

The Great Depression struck Alaska with the same privation as the rest of the country. Across the territory, unemployment soared and there was little new investment. Both Native and non-Native communities endured challenges to their livelihoods and futures. As it did in the rest of the country, the federal government stepped in, making it possible for people to stay in the territory. The Alaska Railroad undertook an austere program of survival. The iron-willed manager, Col. Otto Ohlson, eliminated local tracks he considered expendable, pared the schedule, and maintained high freight rates, all of which earned him the enmity of the populations of Anchorage, Fairbanks, and Seward. Ohlson even lobbied Congress to impose tolls on the government-maintained Richardson Highway so as to insure that Alaska Railroad rates would be competitive.

Federal support, manifest in innovative "New Deal" programs, was substantial. In a number of communities, the Public Works Administration and the Civil Works Administration undertook heavy construction projects. These included a new federal building in Anchorage, a cross-channel bridge in Juneau, a major breakwater in Cordova, and many others. CWA loans helped with construction of a new municipal government building in Anchorage and the rebuilding of the business district of Nome following a disastrous fire in 1934. A dozen Civilian Conservation Corps camps were established in the territory. In southeast, CCC rangers built Forest Service cabins and trails. In south central, they cleared rights-of-way for road construction. In the interior, they fought fires. Some Federal Emergency Relief Agency funds were spent as well. In a number of Alaska villages the Bureau of Indian Affairs brought in supplies to supplement subsistence resources. The Alaska Road Commission undertook a program to construct airfields at various locations to support both mining enterprises and the fledging aviation industry.

But by far the most spectacular New Deal program was the development of a rural rehabilitation colony in the Matanuska Valley near Anchorage. Two hundred families were selected from central and upper Wisconsin and Minnesota to establish farms in Alaska. They would purchase their land with low interest loans, payable when their crops became viable. The colonists were transported by the government to Seattle and from there to Anchorage, every step of their journey eagerly followed by national journalists. Most wrote of new pioneers who would live out the American frontier saga. Direct and overt subsidization by the government seemed not to diminish the perception that these pioneers were latter-day descendants of the rugged settlers who had "opened" the American West.

But generally, the project failed. The government's long-term objectives were to increase non-Native settlement in Alaska and to help the flagging economy, as well as to move Alaska toward agricultural self-sufficiency. The project achieved none of these things, though some colony families own their original farms today and successfully market some crops. But most colonists eventually left the valley. The most significant impediment to the project's success was alternative employment. Just five years after its onset, the U.S. began the remilitarization of Alaska. An Army base and Army Air Service facility were constructed at Anchorage, which became the headquarters of the Alaska Defense Command after the Japanese attack on Pearl Harbor. Colonists found good-paying jobs in civilian construction, both for the government and in the private sector. Most took advantage of the opportunity for faster, bigger money.

❧ ❧

Reorganization of the Indian Office in Alaska and the implementation of a new national Indian policy presented a new front on which Alaskans were able to attack the federal government in the 1930s and 1940s. Somewhat ironically, Alaska Native leaders exacerbated the attack. In 1934 Congress passed the Indian Reorganization Act (IRA), which recognized the right of Indian self-determination and committed the executive branch to protecting Indian self-government, recovering Indian lands, and guaranteeing access to subsistence resources. The act also included a revolving loan fund to support Indian-owned businesses.

As originally passed, the IRA excluded Alaska. This recognized the distinct circumstances of Alaska Natives: no treaties and no reservations. Alaska Natives were distinct in another respect as well: for most Indians in the contiguous states, the tribe was the principal unit of identity and social organization, but in Alaska the exogamous clan was the primary unit. Representing the ANB and other Alaska Natives, William Paul spent several months in Washington, D.C., working with Interior Department and BIA officials, as well as Alaska's new delegate to Congress, Democrat Anthony Dimond, to fashion legislation which would bring the act to Alaska. The result was passage in 1936 of the Alaska Reorganization Act. As finally crafted, it was virtually identical to the IRA, save that the acting collective unit would not be a tribe, but any Alaska Native group with a historic "common bond or association."

By this time, William Paul's political career had ended. In truth, he was a difficult person to work with. He was arrogant and domineering and gained a reputation for rapacity and mendacity. That made it easier for his enemies to organize against him, which they did. Paul's political career did not survive the onslaught this time. On the eve of his second re-election in 1928, one opponent released to the newspapers information that Paul had accepted campaign contributions from cannery companies, though he had attacked them for their use of highly efficient fish traps, which caught so many fish as to eliminate Indians from the fishery. Paul tried to explain that the money was for a lobbying trip to Washington, D.C., for a bill that probably wouldn't affect the number or location of the traps, but such nuances were lost on the electorate. He was finished as an elected politician. But he was not finished in the ANB, which elected him its president within days of the election. Nor did he cease his work as lawyer or editor, and he continued to lobby for passage of the IRA Alaska amendments.

When these amendments passed in Congress, Paul returned to the territory, hoping to make the ANB a business corporation that could process all of the loan fund money for the territory. This was unacceptable to those who distrusted him. They approached the U.S. Attorney in southeast Alaska, who petitioned the court for disbarment of Paul on charges of ethical misconduct. As Paul was traveling with a senate subcommittee taking testimony on Indian conditions in Alaska, he was served a subpoena.

The charges were serious, including several instances of embezzlement of funds. They were made more egregious by the fact that the victims were Indian clients. Paul did not answer the charges and a year later, in 1937, he was disbarred in Alaska. Though the disbarment further diminished his stature and effectiveness, he continued to work on behalf of Indian causes. Among other things, he helped to launch a landmark land claim that became the basis of modern Native land holdings in Alaska, and through the claims settlement act, the legislative context of oil development and federal land conservation in modern Alaska.

In the meantime, the Interior Department and the BIA addressed the conditions and circumstances of Alaska Natives. Historian Kenneth Philp has written that Indian Commissioner John Collier's attempt to implement the IRA in Alaska fomented racism and retarded Native development. Because they were independent of the Indian Office and any federal support save schools and infirmaries, Alaska Natives rejected the idea of Indian reservations, fearing the dependencies they represented. Paul argued to the ANB that reservations were possible without those dependencies, but the organization remained unpersuaded, as did most other Native groups in Alaska, even though the Interior Department had previously established half a dozen small reserves around villages. But the Indian Office pressed ahead with a plan for reservations anyway, both to protect Indian land title and to provide support for needy Indians. Collier wanted to establish small reservations around all the Native villages; he thought this was the surest way to insure the perpetuity of Indian title.

As it developed, there was another way. In 1935 Paul and Dimond lobbied through Congress a bill authorizing the Tlingit and Haida Indians to sue in the U.S. Court of Claims for ownership of all of the land in southeast Alaska, over seventeen million acres. Former judge and delegate James Wickersham had worked out the theory behind the bill in 1929. The Indians would claim the land on the basis of aboriginal title. Congress had extinguished aboriginal title in the contiguous states by the treaties negotiated with Indian tribes, often under fraudulent circumstances. It had extinguished aboriginal title in the Alaska panhandle by creation of the Tongass National Forest between 1902 and 1909, but without compensation. Since compensation was customary in such cases, Wickersham theorized that the Indians could sue for the compensation.

The Tlingit-Haida Jurisdictional Act provided that should compensation be awarded, it should be paid to a "central council" of the Indians, not to individuals. In addition, the act authorized the Indians to retain attorneys to pursue the suit, the selection subject to Interior Department approval. No central council existed when the bill was enacted. Paul decided to make the ANB the central council, and to have his two sons, just then completing law school at the University of Washington, hired as the attorneys. Both parts of the scheme were unacceptable to a majority of the ANB leadership, setting off a power struggle with the Pauls. When it was over, a separate central council had been established, but Paul's sons were retained as attorneys, with the provision that they work in conjunction with an experienced Indian claims attorney. Continuing strife between the Pauls and the ANB delayed the suit for a number of years.

In the meantime, the Indian Office pushed ahead with its plan of establishing new reservations. About two hundred Athabaskan Indians at Tetlin Lake on the Upper Tanana River made their livelihood from trapping, but their area had long been over-trapped by encroaching whites, and they were destitute and in desperate need of help. In 1931 the new BIA Juneau Area Office recommended that a temporary reservation be established for these Indians so Bureau personnel could train them in fur farming, particularly in raising mink. The Office asked that 768,000 acres be set aside, and corrals and pens built. There would be no superintendency on the reservation, though a resident agent would advise the Indians on how to re-establish the population of fur-bearers. Secretary Wilbur agreed, and the reserve was established before the end of the year.

The establishment of a new Indian reservation set off alarm bells within the Alaska Native Brotherhood, for reservations clearly suggested wardship. But the absence of a superintendency suggested the Indian Office might understand Alaska Natives' anxiety. If citizenship guaranteed Indian control on the reservation, Paul argued in the pages of *Alaska Fisherman*, and if the Interior Department defined clearly what activities could and could not be carried out on such land, then establishment of a reservation need not affect Native civil rights, and its creation might dedicate land solely for Indian uses. This was a revolutionary idea, one that generated some discussion in the Interior Department. But because ANB officers could not extract from the BIA the kind of assurances they desired regarding Indian freedom in regard to reservations, the organization ultimately opted to oppose their creation.

Most non-Native Alaskans already knew that they did not want Indian reservations created in Alaska. Protests to creation of the Tetlin Reserve were swift and sweeping. If the government's power to restrict land were not vigorously opposed, Alaskans could expect more restrictions on usable land in the near future, critics asserted. A merchant in Fairbanks wrote to the governor that Alaskans might as well "kiss their freedom good-bye," for soon all in Alaska would be living "in federal peonage." Several writers protested the "blatant discrimination" represented by taking land out of circulation for a special class. Up to now the Indians had been treated as equals, but the government now proposed to elevate a "few hundred uncivilized, unmotivated beggars" above hard-working, "honest Alaskans" who depended on their own "discipline and guts" to supply their own needs.

These arguments were not new in Alaska, but they had seldom been so angrily expressed, except perhaps during the fight over the voters' literacy act in 1924 and 1925. But as John Collier's Indian Bureau, and the Interior Department under New Deal appointee Harold Ickes, addressed the circumstances of Alaska Natives more comprehensively, systematically, and effectively, non-Native protest grew apace. The issue in the 1930s was more the development of an Alaska economy than it was racism. But for many racism lay just under the surface. It might leap forth at any time, as future developments would demonstrate.

Soon after his disbarment in 1937, William Paul took a job as a BIA field agent, counseling villagers on writing IRA village constitutions and forming village governing counsels. As villagers ratified their constitutions, the Indian Office urged them to file for reservations, both to protect the title to the land around the village, and to give councils some control over their own affairs. By 1938 three villages had done so. One application came from Chandalar, a small village north of Fort Yukon, not far west of the Canadian border in the interior. As at Tetlin, increasing numbers of whites had been coming into the region, trapping furbearers the Indians relied on to purchase rifles, traps, coffee, flour, and other goods that were becoming village necessities. Taking the Indian Office at its word as wishing to protect Native lands, the Chandalar Natives asked for a large reservation: 1,408,000 acres. The Juneau Area Office of the BIA, which processed the application, approved it. In Washington, officials expressed caution. A reservation of 640 or 1,200 acres was one thing. Closing nearly a million and a half Alaska acres to mineral exploration and to potential white settlement was quite another.

Another 1938 application with equally significant implications came from Karluk, a village on the north side of Kodiak Island. The Indian Office itself had urged the Karluk people to submit the petition. The waters off their village, at the mouth of the Karluk River, were one of the most productive salmon fisheries anywhere. Each year, however, hundreds of whites fished these waters, and canneries hired additional whites to operate beach seines. The Native Aleuts had been crowded out of their own fishery, and sought work in the nearby canneries. The Indian Office sought to protect the Indians and their resource by recommending a reservation that included the water three thousand feet into the ocean from the beach in front of the village. The notion of a right to the waters off shore was a new one. Fisheries in America had always been treated as a commons, a resource open to anyone. But the Interior Department Solicitor Nathan Margold found that the IRA included language that provided for exclusive Native use of offshore waters based on aboriginal title. On that basis the Karluk Natives asserted an exclusive claim, stating that they had utilized their fishery from "time immemorial."

Cannery operators and investors understood the potential impact of that finding, and its application to Karluk, quite clearly. If the reservation were approved, Natives throughout Alaska might gain approval of similar reservations, giving them an exclusive right to fish, at the very least forcing the canneries to lease seasonal access to the resource. The industry was not about to relinquish its control of the fishery without a fight.

Indian Commissioner Collier and Secretary of the Interior Harold Ickes proceeded on the two applications, approving them on May 20 and May 22, 1943. Non-Native Alaskans reacted negatively to both, though the reaction to the Chandalar reserve was muted since the land affected was hundreds of miles from any urban area, and the only whites affected were those who flew into the region to trap seasonally. Among officials of the canned salmon industry, however, the reaction to the Karluk reservation was immediate and studied. The president of the Alaska Packers' Association wrote that if an exclusive right of Natives to salmon were to be approved for Karluk, it "would gradually spread to other areas" in Alaska. "Our first consideration," he advised, "is blocking the establishment of Indian reservations." Following approval of the reservation, the village council authorized buoys to be set that delineated the area closed to white fishermen. The fishermen ignored the buoys. The next year, the village council adopted an ordinance requiring white fishermen to have permits. The whites fished without them. The next season, the Fish and Wildlife Service issued a regulation requiring non-villagers to obtain permits from Karluk village. At that point, the canners asked a judge to intervene to prevent enforcement of the regulation, which he did. Then the cannerymen filed a lawsuit that eventually went to the U.S. Supreme Court, where the government, and the Natives, lost.

In the meantime, the residents of Hydaburg in southeast Alaska requested a reservation for their village, one that would include adjacent waters, where the village owned and operated a cannery. Two other villages, Kake and Klawock, were considering similar applications when, in 1944, Secretary Ickes decided to ask an administrative law judge to determine whether the Natives of these three villages did in fact have aboriginal rights to the fisheries by their villages. He selected a former justice of the New Mexico Supreme Court to hold hearings on the issue and to render a decision. Ickes intended this review to be a test of the issue of Native lands rights in Alaska.

The Hanna hearings, held in September and November 1944, in the three villages, in Ketchikan, and in Seattle, elicited a violent reaction across southeast Alaska. The canned salmon industry hired top attorneys to present evidence and argue that if the Indians were granted an exclusive right to their fisheries, the industry would be ruined. White leaders picked up the refrain. "Sixty percent of territorial revenue was generated by taxation of the salmon pack over the last seven years," territorial senator Norman Walker testified. If the Natives' right was approved, the territory would lose that revenue. Alaska pioneers would be forced to abandon the territory. An Alaska Miners' Association spokesman said mining claims would have to be abandoned. The head of the Alaska Machinists' Union said six hundred fifty people would be thrown out of work. The president of the Ketchikan Chamber of Commerce said that no pulp mill would ever be established in Alaska, a proposition then under discussion, if the Indians' aboriginal title were found to be legitimate. The Juneau *Daily Alaska Empire* heightened the anxiety with a story titled, "Whole Town of Juneau, Including Gold Mine, Now Claimed by Indians." Its racial bias seemed palpable. In one of his many comments on the issue, *Empire* editor William R. Carter wrote that if Indian title were approved, "All Alaskans will get it in the neck!" He then wrote an open letter to Interior Secretary Harold Ickes that generated a testy response, printed in the *Washington Post*.

Indians testified at the hearings that their ancestors had used the fishery since "aboriginal times," and had been forced out by the whites. The Pauls testified that they wanted a livelihood that could be afforded by owning their own cannery. Other Natives said they wanted to lease the right to fish, traps, and canneries on Indian land to existing producers. The atmosphere at the hearings was tense, particularly in Ketchikan and Seattle, and they were a trial for some of the Indians. Samuel Johnson, a Christian Indian minister from Sitka, wrote to William Paul, Sr., after his testimony that "there is a significant prejudice against us Indians at these hearings."

In the end, the hearings helped to save the fishery for the industry. In his finding, issued in 1945, Hanna found that the Indians had failed to demonstrate that they had used the fishery exclusively. Nor had they charged the whites who had fished in their waters. They had abandoned the fishery and cannery sites to the whites by not officially protesting their appropriation, Hanna wrote. Only in the areas the Indians currently utilized for food, excluding waters, did they have any exclusive right. Secretary Ickes issued an opinion in July granting reservations of 101,000 acres for Hydaburg, 95,000 for Klawock, and 77,000 for Kake, excluding any rights to the offshore waters. Villagers at Klawock and Kake rejected the reservations, and though the people at Hydaburg approved, the U.S. Supreme Court found later, in a suit brought by the salmon industry, that the reserve had been faultily established. The Tlingit-Haida land claims suit would soon be filed in the U.S. Court of Claims to determine if those Indians had title to all the lands of southeast Alaska at the time of the U.S. purchase, and whether the taking of the land through creation of the Tongass National Forest had extinguished their title. But until that court ruled on those questions, Judge Hanna's decision determined the extent of Indian land title in the forest.

Both Collier and Ickes retired soon after the Hanna hearings, leaving the Interior Department's plan for establishing new reservations in Alaska in shambles. Whites in Alaska had won another round in proclaiming the legitimacy of their appropriation of Native lands and resources.

$$\text{\Large \Yo \Yo}$$

The Hanna hearings had elicited derogatory and negative commentary about Alaska Natives, revealing white Alaskans to be still as racist in their attitudes as people anywhere else in America at the time. Wartime circumstances in Alaska exacerbated the subordinate status of Natives in the territory. General Simon Bolivar Buckner was head of the Alaska Defense Command during the war, the supreme commander in the theater. In his reconstruction of the territorial legislature's adoption of an anti-discrimination law in 1945, historian Terrence Cole characterized Buckner as holding "racial views in the 1940s that were little different from those of any rabid Southerner during the Civil War." Buckner issued orders prohibiting soldiers from fraternizing with Native women. He did not want, he said, his soldiers to leave a "mongrelized" population behind as a consequence of serving in Alaska. The only problem with race relations, he averred, was agitators who saw no difference between "the Chinese, the Caucasians, the Japs, the Negroes, the Papuans, the Indians and the Australian bushmen," and would be happy to intermarry with any of them." Buckner went so far as to post off limits any establishments that catered to both Natives and non-Natives. As a result, there was a sharp increase in Anchorage, Buckner's headquarters, of signs reading "Native Trade Not Solicited."

A particularly egregious example of racial discrimination in Alaska involved Aleutian Islanders. In June 1942, Japanese soldiers invaded and conquered the Near Island group at the far west end of the Aleutian Chain, and Kiska and several smaller islands in the Rat Island group. Forty Aleut Natives and a white man and woman, both schoolteachers, were taken prisoner. The male teacher was shot within a few days. The Japanese interned the captives at Otaru City on Hokkaido. Only twenty-four Aleuts and the white woman survived the captivity. The invasion had been essentially a diversionary tactic; the Japanese hoped to divert U.S. Pacific naval forces from the approaching battle of Midway. In response, the American government evacuated the remaining Aleutian Islands, and the Pribilof Islands in the Bering Sea. Though various agencies had earlier discussed an Aleut evacuation, officials had developed no complete plan. Thus, the villagers had to be evacuated under emergency conditions, to remove them from harm's way.

The U.S. government transported 881 villagers to four abandoned canneries in southeast Alaska for the duration of the war. The conditions were atrocious. Preparations had not been made for the evacuees' arrival. The buildings were in disrepair; there was no water dispersal system, no sewage disposal system, and no way to partition the barracks buildings to provide gender or family privacy. Moreover, there were no medical personnel on hand and meager food provisions. The Aleuts were left chiefly to fend for themselves, though government personnel did monitor their situation. Certainly the exigencies of war played a role in these deplorable circumstances. But clearly racism played a role, as well, for it is impossible to imagine that nearly nine hundred white people removed from a war zone would have been treated so shabbily; nor would they have tolerated it if they had been. Medical officers who visited the camps complained to authorities about the conditions, but with little effect.

To add insult to injury, in 1943 and 1944 the government transported hunting parties back to the Pribilof Islands for the annual seal harvest. The Japanese were isolated on Attu and Kiska until May 1943 when a combined American and Canadian force recaptured Attu and the enemy abandoned Kiska. From then until the armistice there was neither action nor threat in the Aleutians. But instead of returning the Aleut Islanders to their homes, the government detained them in Southeast until war's end. Eventually, some of those housed near Juneau and Ketchikan sought work in those towns. But they were discriminated against, like all Alaska Natives, and while they welcomed the opportunity to get out of the camps temporarily, those camps were still their homes. Over forty Aleuts died while the islanders were interned in Southeast Alaska, mostly children and elderly, and many families blamed the deaths on the circumstances in the camps. Meanwhile, back in the islands, military personnel looted Aleut homes and churches, dumped gravel and garbage in salmon streams, and otherwise despoiled Aleut property. The U.S. Navy burned several villages after the evacuation to deny the use of village buildings to the enemy should the Japanese land. Finally, following the war, the islanders were allowed to return, but for many, not to their original villages. Instead, those from a number of the smaller villages were forced to integrate into larger ones.

The prejudicial nature of Alaska society was manifest in other ways during and after the war. In 1947, for example, Congress, federal officials in the territory, and Alaska political leaders were happy to ignore Tlingit and Haida land claims in their pursuit of economic development in the Tongass National Forest. The agency of this example of discrimination was the U.S. Forest Service, and particularly, Alaska's chief forester.

Gov. B. Frank Heintzleman, advocate of forest development. (Courtesy Alaska State Library: Alaska Purchase Centennial Commission Collection)

B. Frank Heintzleman was proud to be an Alaskan. A career forester, he graduated from the Yale School of Forestry in 1910, and came to Alaska in 1918 as a deputy superintendent on the Tongass National Forest. The rest of his career was spent in Alaska. In 1937 he was made Regional Forester of the Alaska Forest Region, in which post he would serve until 1953. In that year President Eisenhower appointed him Alaska's last territorial governor.

A classic Progressive forester, Heintzleman believed that a tree uncut was a tree wasted. He also believed Alaska had no chance for statehood unless its economic base could be broadened. Understanding that expansion meant attracting more outside capital investment in the extraction of Alaska's natural resources, he thought he had the answer: development of Tongass timber. As early as 1927 he wrote that the development of pulp mills on the Tongass would be a basis for the permanent economic development of Alaska. Throughout his career he worked to tie national forest policy in Alaska directly to that end.

After World War II both the United States and Canada experienced major housing booms, and at the same time, a newsprint shortage. Heintzleman used the demand to try to jumpstart pulp development on his forest. A number of would-be investors expressed readiness. The Chief Forester announced that five mills would be built in southeast Alaska that would employ directly and indirectly sixty thousand people. Alaska's total population at the time was only one hundred twenty thousand! But Judge Hanna's finding that Natives did have some aboriginal title in southeast Alaska threatened to stop Heintzleman's plan. As Julius Krug, Ickes's replacement as Interior Secretary noted, no attorney "would be willing . . . to assure [a] contractor or his underwriters that the Forest Service had a certainly good title to the timber within the bounds of the Tongass National Forest." At the same time, the Tlingit-Haida Central Council had finally hired an attorney, James Curry of Washington, D.C., to assemble and file the land claim for all of the land in southeast Alaska on behalf of all the Tlingit and Haida people. The Indians did not want any development of the Tongass forest, or at least none that ignored their interests, until that claim had been resolved. The attorney would file the suit with the Court of Claims in October 1947. By then, however, in the summer of that year, the conservative leadership in Congress had decided pointedly to ignore the Indian protest by passing the Tongass Timber Act, which authorized the Interior Secretary to make pulp mill sites available to investors, and ordered the Forest Service to sign fifty-year contracts with pulp companies and undertake timber lease sales.

Native ownership need not necessarily have precluded economic development, for the Natives were quite capable of leasing their resources or entering into joint ventures with those willing to develop the timber. And such an approach would have been consistent with a turn in Indian policy being undertaken by Congress at that very time. But Heintzleman did not look upon Alaska's Tlingit and Haida as competent people, and neither did most Alaska leaders, and they opposed the Tlingit and Haida protest.

In 1943 the territorial legislature had voted down a proposed anti-discrimination act. In fact, Alaska was "Jim Crow" country; bars and other commercial establishments posted signs proclaiming "No Dogs or Indians Allowed," or the more subtle, "We Reserve the Right to Refuse Service." In Nome, the military supported segregation of the town's only theater. An expanded legislature did pass an anti-discrimination act in 1945, but historian Terrence Cole argues that the act did not end racism in Alaska. In the debate, Elizabeth Peratrovich, president of the Alaska Native Sisterhood, had been chastised by a senator who suggested that a people "barely out of savagery" had considerable nerve in protesting discrimination. Peratrovich retorted that she hadn't thought people with five hundred years of recorded history would need to be reminded of the Bill of Rights.

Governor Ernest Gruening and Congressional Delegate "Bob" Bartlett shared Heintzleman's perception that economic development was critical to Alaska's future, particularly for statehood; it was the foremost principle that drove their thinking about Alaska's future. They also shared the Chief Forester's determination not to turn over land and resources to Indians, though Bartlett supported a compensation award for formal extinguishment of any title the Indians had. Thus, the 1947 Tongass Timber Act set aside Native claims, and provided that all proceeds from timber and land sales would "be maintained in a special account in the Treasury until the rights to the land and timber are finally determined by or under future legislation." The money would be put in escrow, in other words, and development would go forward, "notwithstanding any claim of possessory rights."

Four prominent Native men had flown to Washington at government expense to testify on the Act. Bartlett had arranged the trip, thinking the Indians would support the escrow provision. But in Washington, after a week of meetings with officials in various departments, the group—Frank Peratrovich and Frank Johnson, both on the ANB executive committee; Andrew Hope, elected to the territorial House in 1945; and

Fred Grant, a prominent Haida—concluded that the government simply wanted them out of the way of Alaska's economic development, not as partners. And, they determined, no one was willing to guarantee any Native land title in Alaska. In their testimony, the Indians emphasized the despair felt in the southeast communities over their treatment by the Forest Service and Judge Hanna. People were beginning to change their minds on the matter of reservations, Johnson said, concluding that the limited title so afforded would be better than no title. Fred Grant noted, though, that the Forest Service had issued permits for logging operations on land within the boundaries of the Hydaburg reservation, with no regard for the Indians. Though their remarks were moderate, the four Indians left no doubt that they, and their communities and organizations, opposed the bill. But their remarks had no effect. The bill passed in both the House and the Senate by unanimous consent. President Truman signed the bill on August 8.

A gleeful Forest Service immediately began pitching Alaska timber to potential buyers, and Chief Forester Heintzleman started courting investors for pulp mills. The Indians and their friends protested. The ANB authorized the National Congress of American Indians in Washington, D.C., to print a pamphlet of letters critical of the bill, calling it "an illegal land grab." The title page likened the act to the Teapot Dome scandal of 1924, in which Interior Secretary Albert Fall set aside a national petroleum reserve in Wyoming, and then allowed a private oil company to drill there in return for a payoff. No one was paid off for the Tongass Timber Act, but it did clear the way for pulp development in Alaska. The Ketchikan Chamber of Commerce wrote to the president requesting the pen that had been used to sign the act, and Alaska Governor Gruening wrote to Interior Secretary Krug that Alaska had "had a narrow escape."

Eventually, four fifty-year contracts were let, and investors built two mills. The Ketchikan Pulp Company contract in 1951 led to construction of the Ketchikan plant; the Alaska Pulp Development Company (later, Alaska Pulp Company) contract in 1953 led to the Sitka mill. The Georgia Pacific contract in 1955 led to a sawmill, but the Pacific Northern Timber Company contract was cut back to twenty-five years in 1965 because the company failed to construct a sawmill. Production from the mills proved marketable in a period of remarkable national growth, and the population of southeast Alaska increased significantly. In the meantime, the Court of Claims decided the Tlingit-Haida claims suit in the Indians' favor in 1959, leading to a minimum compensatory award in 1968, on which more will be said later. In 1947, timber for which the Indians would be owed compensation was being harvested without their consent. The logging of the Tongass Forest would be fraught with controversy.

The lesson of the Tongass Timber Act was not lost on Alaska's Native people. For them, Governor Ernest Gruening and Alaska Territorial Delegate "Bob" Bartlett had shown their true colors, colors shared by a majority of non-Native Alaskans. Though both professed commitment to the cause of Native rights and equity, both were nonetheless willing to suppress those rights in favor of Alaska's economic development, which they regarded as critical for Alaska statehood. For both, statehood was a higher cause. Moreover, in this instance, they were quite willing to trust Alaska's economic future to both the federal government and absentee corporate investors. The federal government, through the U.S. Forest Service, would plan and conduct the timber lease sales that would provide the raw resources for the pulp mills. And the pulp mills could only be built and operated by corporations commanding significant financial resources. In time, the people of Alaska would have reason to complain about violations of trust by both entities.

꙳ ꙳

After World War II the quest for statehood would dominate Alaska public policy discussion and action. To provide an irrefutable factual basis from which to construct a campaign to persuade Congress to grant statehood, the territorial legislature placed a referendum on the question on the general election ballot in 1946. The results were encouraging for statehood advocates, 9,634 (58.5 percent) voting in favor, 6,822 against. As the campaign moved forward, Alaskans would come to realize better how inextricably their vision of themselves was bound to the two issues of Native rights and the role of natural resources. As we have seen, the majority of Alaskans understood their future in terms of the development of those resources. Alaska, said a famous booster of the territory, Major Marvin "Muktuk" Marston, was to the generation of 1946 what California had been to the generation of its great gold rush in 1849, "a great undeveloped territory with great wealth." With Forester Heintzleman, Marston took the traditional Progressive Era view of resource development, that a resource undeveloped was an opportunity for economic advance that had been missed.

Gruening and Bartlett believed passionately in Alaska statehood, and they planned a coordinated campaign to end the second-class citizenship of Alaska residents. In 1943 Alaska's Congressional delegate, Anthony Dimond, had introduced an Alaska statehood bill in the House, and when he succeeded Dimond in the 1944 election, Bartlett did the same. In 1946 Gruening asked President Truman to include a recommendation on Alaska in his State of the Union address, which Truman did. But soon afterward he learned that unresolved Native claims were a problem. He urged the Interior Department to "get up a bill which will approach a fair settlement of this unresolved situation."

In the meantime, in Seattle and Alaska, the canned salmon industry began to organize against statehood. The industry probably had no choice but to do so. Statehood would mean closer regulation and probably additional taxation, both of which would erode the profitability of a multi-million dollar enterprise. The industry's champion was W. C. Arnold, chief attorney and lobbyist for the canners' trade association, Alaska Salmon Industry, Inc. A cannery lawyer with twenty-five years of experience, Arnold was a formidable foe. Statehood should be delayed, he argued, until all Native land claims were settled. Like the Forest Service, leaders of the canned salmon industry did not believe Alaska Natives had any land rights; they did not accept the notion of aboriginal title. But in a clear scare tactic, Arnold spelled out an imaginary consequence of the government's potential recognition of such title. "If the Indians have any claims," Arnold opined, "let's have them decided. If they own the country, I think that should be determined so the rest of us can leave." It was ridiculous, he argued, for the Interior Department to advocate settlement of Alaska and at the same time "assert the Indian title to all the real estate and all the fishing grounds in the territory."

In the long run the salmon industry became its own worst enemy, for Arnold's articulate opposition helped turn Alaskans solidly against the canners, and to turn Alaska Salmon Industry, Inc., into a symbol of exploitation and dependence, evils, as Alaskans considered them, that statehood would eradicate. The canneries, the lobbying group, and particularly the Alaska Packers' Association, the largest corporate combine of individual canneries, became together the target of Alaskans' frustrations over continued territorial status and the struggle for statehood.

Statehood advocates used the weapon the industry gave them effectively. In 1954 Democrat Gruening, replaced as governor after Republican Dwight Eisenhower was elected president, published a history of the territory, which he titled *State of Alaska*. The book was designed to make the case for statehood. The former governor penned an exposé of abuse by the canned salmon industry with its notorious fish traps, and by the other nemesis of Alaska, the federal government. Both, he claimed, were villainous tormentors, insensitive and unsympathetic. The one impeded Alaska's development by restricting land use and opportunity; the other exploited the region's most prolific resource, bilking Alaskans of what rightfully belonged to them. Statehood, its advocates argued, would free Alaskans from such abuse, and would give them control over their own destinies, making them independent and free.

Alaskans wanted to be free to generate a larger return from the harvest of their resources. Throughout hearings on statehood held over the decade after 1947, Alaskans repeated one message as if it were a mantra: lack of statehood hinders and impedes Alaska's economic development. No one, as historian Peter A. Coates has noted, attributed Alaska's lack of development to geography, climate, or environment. Rather, federal policy and absentee owner exploitation were the culprits. Left undeveloped, the territory was a wasteland; developed, it would equal California in its rate of population and economic growth. "We are going to build a Fifth Avenue on the tundra," future governor Walter Hickel proclaimed, referring to New York City. But Alaskans were much less clear on what exactly the economic development would be. Minerals and agricultural opportunity headed the list of activities that would supposedly thrive under statehood. Despite the example of the failed Matanuska Colony, many testified that Alaska would become agriculturally self-sufficient under statehood. Various representatives of miners' groups insisted that, with state rather than federal control of land, many more acres would be opened up, and with less restriction, Alaska would produce enough mineral wealth to run the country. But while grandiose in their rhetoric, such claims were usually woefully short on specifics. Virtually no one who testified for statehood attempted to relate a future Alaska economy to market trends or prices, to investment costs, or to transportation networks. Witnesses simply asserted that all of these things would be cheaper and better under statehood. In truth, the principal argument for statehood was the civic and moral one, that Alaskans, fully capable of civic responsibility, should not be denied the same control over their own affairs enjoyed by any citizen of any state of the union.

If the canned salmon industry emerged as the chief villain, federal conservation of Alaska land and resources was not far behind. An early statehood bill written by Delegate Bartlett in 1947 had called for transfer of federal parks and reserves in the territory to the state government. This was a measure of Alaskans' distrust of the federal government and their resentment of federal land withdrawals in the territory. But such provisions alarmed conservationists and responsible land managers throughout federal government and elsewhere. The National Parks Association worried about the impact of statehood on Katmai National Monument, which supported an extensive brown bear population. The CIO Committee on Regional Development and Conservation urged that the national forests, fish and wildlife refuges, and all minerals remain in federal ownership. The Alaska Sportsmen's Council, allied with the National Wildlife Federation, testified that Alaskans' pioneer mentality mandated continued federal control of the territory's natural resources. To counter these voices of national conservation, Gruening organized a one-hundred-member "national committee of distinguished Americans," including many outdoorsmen and even government officials, to lobby for statehood.

The final step in the statehood campaign was the drafting of a state constitution, and its approval by Alaska voters. To this end, in 1955 the Alaska territorial legislature authorized an election for delegates to a constitutional convention. The delegates met for seventy-five days on the campus of the University of Alaska in Fairbanks. Gruening gave the keynote address to the group, which he called "Let Us End Alaska Colonialism." His principal *leitmotif* likened Alaska's territorial status to the American colonies under England's George III and Parliament.

The convention had the benefit of the best consultants on state constitutions who could be attracted to Alaska, or who were willing to write papers, including university experts, private researchers, the National Municipal League, the Legislative Reference Service of the Library of Congress, members of the American Political Science Association, the Institute of Public Administration in New York, the Public Administration Service, and others. The delegates produced a progressive, uncluttered constitution regarded as one of the best of the fifty state constitutions. It would become an important tool in the final phase of the statehood campaign.

The convention's debate on natural resources is of particular interest. Victor Fischer, a university researcher who was elected to the convention, wrote in a 1975 analysis that the delegates strove for a "harmonious balance between consumption, preservation and expansion of natural resources." Delegates placed special emphasis, he said, on management of renewable resources by the principles of sustained yield and multiple use. Bartlett addressed the convention on the subject before the delegates took up their work. His remarks are revealing of how Alaskans saw their future in regard to the environment. Two dangers confronted the state,

Gov. Ernest Gruening, champion of economic development. (Courtesy Alaska State Library: Alaska Purchase Centennial Commission Collection)

he said. The first was "exploitation under the thin disguise of development." What he meant was "the taking of Alaska's mineral resources without leaving some reasonable return for the support of Alaska governmental services and the use of all the people in Alaska." Second, "outside interests," in order to stifle development of Alaska's resources so as not to compete with their activities elsewhere, might seek to acquire control of Alaska's lands "in order NOT to develop them until such time, in their omnipotence and pursuance of their own interests, they saw fit." These statements are remarkable for their understanding of Alaska's dependence on forces beyond its control for its economic future. Bartlett grasped fully that that future lay in resource development. The Alaskans of the future, he told the convention, would likely judge the success of the constitution "not by decisions taken upon issues like local government, apportionment, and the structure and powers of the three branches of government, but rather by the decision taken upon the vital issue of resources policy." But conservation of those resources was not on Bartlett's agenda. Alaskans neither needed nor wanted, he lectured the delegates, a resource policy which "will prevent orderly development of the great treasures" which were theirs.

Just who should benefit from such sustained development? Bartlett told the delegates that the constitution should include a clause similar to that of other state constitutions, mandating that it should be the people, all the people, of the state who should benefit. But, he said, such "pious generalities, without further concrete policy statements, have proved wholly inadequate as effective barriers against dissipation of resources, fraud and corruption." Alaskans should have "effective safeguards" against the exploitation of their resources "by persons and corporations whose only aim is to skim the gravy and get out." In other words, it should be Alaskans who should reap the profits of the development of their resources, not Outsiders.

There was a great deal of naiveté in Bartlett's vision, however, for outside capital investment could only mean substantial outside control. Not much policy can be written into a constitution. And in the end the delegates could not direct the future very comprehensively. Moreover, they could not agree on vital issues among themselves. After wrangling for weeks over whether or not to provide separate commissions to manage fish and game, in order to keep the governor from politicizing their work, they passed the problem to future legislatures, which eventually handed it to the governor. There were similar difficulties regarding minerals. The statehood bills in Congress mandated a leasing regime for mineral development, rather than blanket openings for claims. Congress was so strong on this issue that early bills called for reversion of title from the state to the federal government if that policy was not followed. The reason was that leasing would generate revenue for state administration. But in addition to providing for a leasing regime in the constitution, the delegates added a claims clause. As in the federal system, oil, gas, coal, oil shale, sodium, phosphate, potash, sulfur, pumice, and "other minerals as prescribed by law" would be leased. All others, most notably gold, silver, zinc, copper, lead, and other precious and common metals, would be open to discovery and claim. Delegates transferred responsibility for eliminating discovery to Congress, assuming the solons would change what the Alaskans submitted. However, by the time statehood passed, senators and representatives bowed to history and tradition, and left in the traditional minerals open to exploration and discovery.

On the other issue that occupied the delegates' thinking on natural resources, Native land rights, the convention nearly came to grief. At the beginning of their debate, "Muktuk" Marston urged them to grant title to Natives of all lands they actually occupied and used. This was a moral obligation Alaskans had toward the Natives, he told the delegates. They could write a constitution with "heart and soul and justice in it," he said, by including that one provision. He believed, he said, the convention had "the honor and the justice and the will" to do right by Alaska Natives, something the "United States government has been unable to do." But he was wrong. The convention did not have the will, at least. Though some supported his proposal, most did not. They worried that action by the convention might interfere with Congress's attempts to deal with the issue. Most considered Native lands a federal, not a state, responsibility. Others thought that there should be no special class of Alaskans created, and that therefore land grants should also be made to non-Native Alaskans. But this brought the rejoinder that such a provision would disadvantage future Alaskans. Discussion degenerated into confusion, contradiction, and muddle. In the end, the delegates placed nothing regarding Native land rights in the constitution, making a mockery of Marston's sincere attempt to do justice.

The delegates also ignored any special relationship between Native culture and utilization of fish and game, or any special resource needs Native people might have. In its final version, as approved by Alaska voters, the constitution directed the legislature to provide for the utilization, development, and conservation of all natural resources belonging to the state ". . . for the maximum benefit of its people," a clause which clearly precluded preferential, special, or discriminatory management. This issue would emerge after 1980 to bedevil Alaskans, and to help re-open the rift between Native and non-Native people and interests in the state. The article also mandated that fish, forests, wildlife, grasslands, and all other "replenishable resources" are to be "utilized, developed and maintained on the sustained yield principle, subject to preferences among beneficial users." While ideal in theory, the fact that sustained yield admits of many interpretations, and that preferences can be established by the legislature or perhaps by the fish and game boards (commissions), effectively vitiated the section. Overall, the constitution was more effective in demonstrating what Alaskans thought about the state's natural resources in 1955-56 than it was in establishing effective policies for their management in the future. Alaska voters approved the constitution in spring of 1956.

As the Congress took up Alaska statehood in 1957, Alaskans' attention was momentarily diverted by a spectacular new resource development, one which held the promise not only of paying for the new state, but making it—or at least a few of its residents—independently wealthy. In April 1957, Richfield Oil Co. (soon to merge with Atlantic Oil Company to become ARCO) drilled into a petroleum deposit on the Kenai Peninsula. The well promised to deliver five hundred barrels a day. It was the beginning of the modern oil era in Alaska, though it was clearly a modest beginning.

Richfield's discovery well has entered legend not only because of its role in Alaska's oil boom, but also because of the way in which it was located. The entire Kenai Peninsula was a conservation area, the Kenai National Moose Range, a 1,730-million-acre preserve established in 1941, managed by the U.S. Fish and Wildlife Service to protect the habitat of this largest member of the deer family. The range was not managed as a wilderness, but as protection for wild game. In the post-war population boom in southcentral Alaska, though, Alaskans sought the land in the range for agricultural homesteads, even though its agricultural potential was limited. To Alaskans, protecting moose rather than encouraging settlement was anathema and the Interior Department permitted agricultural entry to the land. Most entries that were filed were not worked. Nonetheless, responding to the same clamor for development, in 1955 the Department granted some leases for oil exploration in the range. It was on one of these that Richfield drilled its discovery well. Because the lease was in a conservation area, the Fish and Wildlife Service only permitted Richfield to detonate one seismic line, a series of small, sonar-analyzed explosions that allow geologists to map an oil prospect, and highly restricted road construction. After analyzing the data and conducting a visual survey, an Alaska oil geologist working for Richfield dug his in heel at what seemed to him the most likely spot to drill a well. "Drill here," he said, and that's where the well came in.

Any thoughts most Anchorage residents had about the moose range after that were of how to get rid of it. Richfield capped their discovery well while they waited for additional leases on the range to pursue more exploration and development. In response to complaints from Alaskans, the Interior Department agreed to open more land in the Range to leasing. The Wildlife Management Institute, the National Wildlife Federation, the Izaak Walton League, the Sport Fishing Institute, the Wilderness Society, and the National Parks Association supported limited leasing under strict controls. Alaskans called loudly for the lifting of all restrictions. In August 1958, Interior Secretary Fred Seaton opened one-half the entire Range to oil exploration. Subsequent oil finds were not substantial. In 1959 attention shifted offshore into Cook Inlet, where both oil and gas were discovered.

The discovery of oil played little or no role in Congress's decision to pass the Alaska statehood bill in 1958. Kenai oil simply was not substantial enough to answer the costs of statehood. Instead, Congress included in the Alaska statehood act a provision obligating payment to Alaska of 90 percent of federal mineral lease revenue collected anywhere in Alaska. The remaining 10 percent of revenue would be used to administer federal public lands in the state. This was an exceedingly generous provision. Congress had routinely dedicated a portion of mineral lease revenue collected in the several states to the state in which it was collected, but normally the amounts ranged from 37.5 to 50 percent. This generosity was consistent with the federal government's supportive role throughout Alaska's development, the most salient example of which, before the statehood act, had been construction and operation of the Alaska Railroad. But had the great Prudhoe Bay oil discovery preceded statehood, it is highly unlikely that any such generosity would have appeared in the statehood act.

⭑⭑

The three decades from the election of Democrat Anthony Dimond as Alaska's delegate to Congress to the passage of the Alaska statehood bill through the U.S. Congress saw Alaska's economic future brighten considerably. From the depths of the Great Depression, when support for Alaska settlement from the federal government was for many non-Natives all that stood between staying in Alaska and returning to the contiguous states, the territory had been the economic beneficiary of military spending during World War II and the onset of the Cold War. As in other parts of the American West, federal spending and construction helped to bring Alaska into the twentieth century. The resulting non-Native population boom generated political pressure for statehood. It also helped to sharpen Alaskans' oppositional habits of thought and reaction, particularly those directed against Natives, and against any who would urge protection of the natural environment.

An Alaskan old-timer, a non-Native, summed up the change in Alaska during these three decades. He was speaking of the impact of World War II, to a war correspondent for a national magazine, but he could as well have been speaking of the period as a whole. "The old Alaska is gone," he said; "she's wrecked." But the shape of the new Alaska was far from clear.

4

Bonanza: Prudhoe Bay and ANCSA

ɞ ᕑ

Alaska entered a new era with the discovery of a deposit of fifteen billion barrels of oil by Atlantic Richfield Corporation (ARCO) at Prudhoe Bay on Alaska's North Slope in 1967 and 1968. The field, 45 miles long by 18 miles wide, was North America's largest discovered oil deposit both by volume and by the amount of recoverable oil. Oil companies stood to make billions of dollars in profit from the find. The State of Alaska also anticipated billions in tax revenue to fund state government. Individual Alaskans hoped to make money from the impending boom associated with development of the field and the oil pipeline to be built to transport the oil across the state to a warm-water port on the Gulf of Alaska. All of these anticipated impacts have been realized at a magnitude greater than even the most optimistic Alaskans dared hope in 1967.

Oil development together with the establishment of the Arctic National Wildlife Refuge (ANWR) fused the issues of Native rights and environmental protection, and made them preeminent in shaping Alaska's economy and its culture. At the time of the Prudhoe Bay discovery, Alaska Native land claims still had not been settled. Industry leaders recognized immediately the challenge this posed for oil development. A pipeline could not be built until Native claims had been cleared, one way or another. That circumstance gave Alaska Natives tremendous leverage, perhaps greater than any other group of Native Americans had ever had in relation to American corporate economic power. Alaska's Native people would not squander that opportunity to provide for their economic future. Beyond economics, the longer-term and broader impact of this power shift is a matter still much under analysis.

Prudhoe Bay State No. 1, the discovery well.
(Courtesy Anchorage Museum of History and Art)

The environment, too, lay in the path of the trans-Alaska pipeline, and oil development in the state. Through a fortuity no fiction writer would dare have scripted, the Prudhoe Bay find lay between two huge federal land withdrawals, one a strategic petroleum reserve, the other America's newest and largest wildlife refuge. Americans' growing concern about environmental preservation gave those Americans interested in wildlife, wilderness, and nature a similar kind of leverage to that enjoyed by the Alaska Natives. The more concerned Americans became about environment, the more they began to look to Alaska as a legacy they could reserve to pass on to future generations, a precious legacy of the wilderness that had covered the landscape before Euro-American development of North America began, and an untrammeled land of unequaled scenic and spiritual beauty and ruggedness.

Most Alaskans reacted predictably to both of these challenges to their cultural assumption that economic development is the preferred, superior use of Alaska's land and resources. They supported the development of Prudhoe Bay, the construction and operation of the pipeline, the building of the receiving, storage, and shipping facility at Valdez at the southern terminus of the pipeline, and the plying of Prince William Sound by oil tankers filled with Alaska crude oil bound for processing and marketing. They resisted with all the tools at their disposal the reservation of any additional conservation areas in the state, and when their creation proved unstoppable, worked to guarantee that known potentials for economic development would not be impeded, and that restrictions on land use would be as limited as they could make them.

The development and prosperity brought by Prudhoe Bay and related oil development exacerbated Alaskans' conflict with Natives and their antagonism toward supporters of the environment, principal among whom was the federal government. Prudhoe Bay prosperity also exacerbated Alaskans' economic dependence on Outsiders, and therefore their economic insecurity. Because nearly all Alaskans, including Natives, wanted economic development in the state, their leaders would have no choice but to become partners with the oil industry. They should do so, Alaskans insisted, in such a way as to protect Alaska's interest. But what was Alaska's interest? Was it more development, less development, the greatest return for extraction of the resource? And how could the state enforce its will on the corporations? Would too much taxation and regulation drive them to curtail production and exploration? Would assiduous accounting and enforcement of the state's demands generate excessive caution or petulance in the industry? And who was to be the arbiter of a fair demand?

Finally, oil prosperity exacerbated Alaskan greed. Acting on the principle that benefit from development of their natural resources stay in Alaska, Alaskans created a publicly owned permanent investment fund from some of the taxes extracted from the oil industry. Some of the earnings of the Alaska Permanent Fund are distributed *per capita* to all Alaska residents annually. In the last decade Alaskans have become politically insistent that none of those earnings be used to pay for regular government services, despite extraordinary budget deficits. Moreover, they have elected a series of conservative legislatures who have acted on the conviction that voters would prefer to forego new taxes rather than increase government services. In the following pages we shall examine and comment on these phenomena, which are, I believe, the essential elements of Alaska's history since statehood.

>◦ ◦<

Famous naturalist Robert Marshall, founder of the Wilderness Society, had spent a year in Alaska in the early 1930s, and on his return had proposed to Congress that all of Alaska north of the Arctic Circle be established as a national wilderness. Though he died in 1939, Marshall's recommendation did not go unnoticed. In 1951 Olaus Murie, who had worked as a researcher for the Bureau of Biological Survey (later the U.S. Fish and Wildlife Service) in Alaska before World War II, renewed the recommendation to the Wilderness Society, of which he was at that time director. Murie noted the effect of the post-war population boom on the remote areas of the region. Soon other private conservation groups, including the Sierra Club, the Izaak Walton League and the Western Federation of Outdoor Clubs, joined the Wilderness Society in recommending study of an Arctic wilderness area. But the initial impetus to examine Marshall's proposal had actually come from the National Park Service, which had dispatched two surveyors to the region in 1949. They coordinated their work with the U.S. Geological Survey and the Office of Naval Research, which had responsibility for the 23.5 million-acre Naval Petroleum Reserve No. 4, established in 1923, between the Arctic Coast and the Brooks Range, from the Colville River west to Icy Cape. In 1954 the Park Service recommended federal protection for the area they had surveyed, the northeast corner of Alaska. In 1959 the Interior Department sent a bill for the proposed refuge to Congress.

Alaskan supporters of the refuge idea founded the Alaska Conservation Society (ACS) in 1959, even as a House committee prepared to hold hearings in Alaska. ACS members argued at the hearings that some portion of the Arctic deserved protection because wilderness areas had inspired the frontier spirit in America, and if there were no reminder left, that spirit would surely die more quickly. As Peter Coates observed, the ACS wanted to preserve "vicarious pioneering." But they also wanted to preserve what they regarded as a fragile and precious ecosystem. A number of highly credible scientists from the University of Alaska in Fairbanks were members of the ACS, and testified in support of the refuge; so did Richard Cooley, a founding member and director of the Alaska Natural Resource Center. These experts outlined for the House committee the notion of ecosystem, perhaps the first use of the concept in a political context in Alaska. All of the natural systems within the region were linked in a harmonious balance, they argued, including all the flora and fauna. Though such testimony was impressive for conservationists, most Alaskans believed the proposed reserve was "worthless land." But no newspaper opposed creation of the refuge, and in 1960 the House passed the refuge bill.

Olaus Murie took the lead in lobbying the bill through the Senate, but did not succeed. Gruening and Bartlett, elected Alaska's first two U.S. senators, opposed the bill steadfastly. Bartlett chaired the committee that handled the bill, and he killed it without extensive discussion. But Secretary of the Interior Fred Seaton had already decided to recommend creation of the reserve by executive order, under the provisions of the 1906 Antiquities Act. To make the withdrawal more palatable, he paired the order with rescission of a World War II order that had made all of the territory north of the Brooks Range a temporary military reserve. Gruening denounced the refuge order as a violation of states' rights, a callous disregard of promises in the statehood act entitling the state to select vacant and unreserved lands. The Alaska legislature adopted a resolution calling on the new president to review and rescind Seaton's order. But Kennedy's new Interior Secretary, Stewart Udall, supported the idea of the wildlife refuge, and so let the executive order stand.

Historian Peter Coates concludes that creation of the nineteen-million-acre Arctic National Wildlife Refuge (ANWR) opened a twenty-year struggle for protection of wilderness, frontier, and ecological values in Alaska that culminated in the Alaska National Interest Lands Conservation Act (ANILCA) of 1980. As we shall see, the rhetoric in that struggle verged on the hysterical as the state's entitlement for a portion of Alaska's land was delayed while other claimants made their selections. An important contribution of the debate over ANWR was the introduction of the notion of an ecosystem to the American public. Ecology had been an esoteric area of biological studies before the Alaska lands debate. By the time the lands bill passed the Congress in 1980, most Americans had heard the term, and most thought they knew what it meant.

The American scientific community learned a great deal about ecology, and about biological linkage, from another Alaskan incident that had the potential to become an ecological disaster, Project Chariot. In 1957 the Atomic Energy Commission (AEC) undertook a project code-named Ploughshare to investigate "peaceful uses of the atom," nonmilitary applications of nuclear detonations, especially in heavy construction. Because the Alaskan Arctic was "empty land," i.e., scarcely inhabited, AEC officials selected a site near Point Hope on the Arctic coast north of Kotzebue for a test. The AEC proposed excavating a harbor and access channel capable of handling ocean cargo vessels. The project would have little economic utility; after initial discussions, it was identified chiefly as an experiment. But the AEC anticipated spending $5 million on the endeavor, and attracting another $5 million from private industry. State officials were not enthusiastic about the project, though they did not oppose it. Business people in Alaska, however, were highly supportive of the idea. Chambers of commerce and newspaper editors touted its economic benefit as a one-time infusion of needed money, and hoped long-term economic benefits might be found later. Environmental protest and growing distrust of the AEC eventually led officials to abandon the project in 1963.

Chariot had several important effects on the development of Alaska and its culture. First, it sharply focused the attention of the national environmental scientific community on Alaska. Fallout was just emerging as a national public health concern at this time. Chariot offered a tangible, easily understood object lesson on the danger of fallout, as well as helping to educate scientists and others on the point of biological linkage. But more pertinent to Alaska, Chariot helped dispel the notion that the Alaskan Arctic was an empty land and, with the establishment of ANWR, helped to popularize the understanding of the Arctic environment as biologically rich, diverse, and fragile. Second, protest over the project provided a context for the coalescing of conservationists in Alaska. From Chariot forward, ACS would be a significant player in environmental debate about Alaska. The project also helped to solidify contact and communication between ACS and national environmental groups, alliances that would be critical in the environmental battles ahead. Finally, Chariot helped to provide focus for new Native organization in the state. Eskimo leaders from across the Arctic met in Barrow in 1961 to form Inupiat Paitot, an Eskimo political body. Among other things, the group recommended the founding of a statewide Native newspaper. Within a year, they were able to begin publication of *Tundra Times*, which played a significant role in raising Native consciousness, and in the struggle for Native land rights that lay ahead. Especially noteworthy for this study, however, is the role played by Alaska business leaders and civic leaders. As in the debate over the Tongass Timber Act in 1947, their commitment to economic development overshadowed all other considerations.

Advocates of development were even more vigorous and uncompromising in their support of another project that promised economic benefits for Alaska at about the same time, Rampart Dam. In 1954 the U.S. Army Corps of Engineers, in competition with the Bureau of Reclamation in building hydroelectric, irrigation, and flood-control dams in the American West, began to assess the feasibility of a major dam on the Yukon River at the downstream end of a natural 100-mile gorge called Rampart Canyon. The canyon lies just downstream of the Yukon Flats area, a lowland of lakes and muskeg that the U.S. Fish and Wildlife Service estimated was the summer habitat of 1.5 million migratory waterfowl. Primarily a hydroelectric dam, the facility would produce 4.77 million kilowatts of power. The reservoir behind the dam would fill the Yukon Flats area, creating a body of water larger in surface area than Lake Erie, 200 miles long and between 40 and 90 miles wide. Six Native villages would be flooded, their residents relocated to new sites. The reservoir would take twenty years to fill.

Nearly all Alaska leaders supported the Rampart project. Senator Gruening made it a personal crusade, lobbying intensely for it in Congress, with the Interior Department, and in Alaska until he was defeated for reelection to the Senate in 1968. Bartlett, though less enthusiastic, helped to develop and sustain support until his untimely death by heart attack in the same year. Virtually all the chambers of commerce and newspaper editors in the state supported it. The Alaska legislature passed several resolutions in its favor, and appropriated money to advertise its supposed benefits to Alaska.

The greatest opposition to Rampart came from an American populace that was in the process of adopting environmentalism as a national resource policy. In the late 1950s and early 1960s Americans embraced a new determination to protect nature, both in a practical context related to safety, as in clean air and water, and in an ideal context, as in new national parks and wilderness preserves. When Rachael Carson in her 1962 book, *Silent Spring*, warned of technology's betrayal, showing the relationship between DDT spraying and the disappearance of songbirds, Americans were ready for the message. And when Interior Secretary Stewart Udall, in *Quiet Crisis* in 1963, added his voice to the many already calling for preservation of the country's remaining wilderness, Americans heard the call and widely began to support protectionist legislation.

Environmental opposition to the Rampart Dam project lay chiefly in its impact on cultural values, i.e., on Native life and its relation to the land, and on the planned destruction of a valuable, complex ecosystem, an example of pristine ecology. Native dissent played an important role in the final decision to cancel the project. Coates found that Alaska supporters of the project could not understand the environmental protest. The land that would be affected had no special scenic value. The waterfowl could swim in one place as well as another, they thought (an incorrect assumption). And Natives also could subsist in one place on the river as well as another, a gross failure to understand the concept of place in traditional and contemporary identity, as well as the validity of Native land rights. Rampart nicely illustrates the degree to which Alaskans were out of step with the shift in national consciousness. Bob Bartlett was the only Alaskan leader whose comments showed that he understood that a sea change was taking place in America, and that Alaska would reap the whirlwind. For the others, events ahead would hold a rude awakening.

⊱ ⊰

Most Alaskans expected that statehood would free Alaska, that it would bring independence, development, control, and prosperity. It brought none of these, at least not to the extent anticipated. Too few appreciated the role of absentee capital, of global market forces, and of federal sovereignty in limiting state options. And many Alaskans missed the full spectrum of two enormous changes in American culture in the 1950s and 1960s: respect for the equality of minorities and for the environment. Alaskans understood that changes were taking place. One could not watch television, even the "canned" variety that Alaskans had access to before 1971, or read a major urban newspaper, and not see the shift in consciousness on civil rights. Alaskans even noted such legislation as the clean air and water acts, and the migratory waterfowl and migratory mammal protection acts of the 1960s, with general approval. But they failed to mark the depth of the changes, and as a result were unprepared for their consequences for the new state.

There was a significant conflict embedded in the Alaska statehood act. Section 6 of the act entitled the new state to select from "vacant, unappropriated and unreserved land" approximately 104 million acres of Alaska's 375 million acres as state lands, about 28 percent of the land base. As a percentage, 28 percent was not much. But in terms of acreage, it was huge, bigger than the entire state of California. The reason for such a large entitlement, whose size concerned many members of Congress, was to provide economic resources to the state, particularly mineral resources that could be leased for revenue. But the state's entitlement was potentially inconsistent with section 4 of the act, a disclaimer of "all right and title" to any lands that might be subject to Native right or title. If William Paul was correct in thinking that Alaska Natives still held their traditionally utilized lands by aboriginal title, then, as noted above, most of the land in Alaska might be subject to Native title. "Takings" by the federal government at the time of statehood totaled about 54 million acres.

A few Alaskans did understand the implications of the two sections of the statehood act, and more would come to understand them shortly. Alaska would officially become the 49th state of the union on January 3, 1959, and state planners set about plotting the state's selection of the 104 million acres provided in the statehood act, assuming that the disclaimer was a statement of principle, not the letter of the law. The work moved swiftly, and soon the state began to file applications with the Bureau of Land Management (BLM). Officials in that agency were sympathetic to the state's desire quickly to gain control of land that might have economic potential. By 1965 the BLM had assigned provisional title to the state of about twelve million acres.

As the state began to make selections, however, Natives protested. Aided by officials of the Association of American Indian Affairs (AAIA), and by Bureau of Indian Affairs attorneys, Native villages and individuals began to file protests to the state's selections. Veteran national Indian claims attorneys advised from a distance. On their advice, Natives began also to assemble their own claims to Alaska land, based on the principle of aboriginal title, as well as actual use and occupation.

At the same time, the wealthy publisher Dr. Henry Forbes, a member of the AAIA board, decided to fund a Native newspaper. Enthusiasm ran high in the Arctic Slope communities after the initial meeting of Inupiat Paitot. But there was no communication medium or mechanism to extend that conversation, and utilize what Natives were learning collectively. And what they were learning was eye opening. Eskimos from widely separated villages found they had been treated with similar shabbiness by white organizations. A special target of their complaints was the BLM, which had granted the AEC a permit for use of one million acres of land on the west Arctic coast for Project Chariot without consulting with affected Natives. Now, that same agency was summarily denying Native protests to state land selections. At the same time, the new state government was ignoring their claims and protests. The Eskimo newspaper Forbes funded, called *Tundra Times,* became a major catalyst for Native action, as well as a clearinghouse for information. Forbes had gotten to know Eskimo artist Howard Rock, a brilliant, plainspoken, modest man committed to Alaska Native rights and dignity. Forbes and others persuaded Rock to edit the paper. Rock used his courageous editorials to define and defend Native rights. He quickly became a voice all Alaska listened to. And his calls to action produced results.

New regional Native organizations emerged among most Native groups, and in 1965 three hundred delegates from Tlingit and Haida, Athabaskan, Eskimo, and Aleut villages and from the state's white towns met in Anchorage to plan a new statewide Native organization, the Alaska Federation of Natives. The AFN would become the voice of Native Alaska, and Natives and whites of diverse points of view would unite under its banner and work for a united position on issues affecting Natives.

In the meantime, officers in the state office of the BLM rejected all of the protests that came to them. Native leaders did not know what the next step should be. The AAIA suggested Ted Stevens, known to be sympathetic to Native rights. A decorated war veteran, Stevens had served as U.S. Attorney in Fairbanks, 1953-56, and as legislative counsel and assistant to the Secretary of the Interior, 1956-60; he was Solicitor in the Interior Department, 1960-61. He entered private practice in Fairbanks in 1961, running unsuccessfully for U.S. Senate in 1962. He was thoroughly familiar with Alaska Native affairs, and more important, with the implications of the disclaimer section in the statehood act. He deplored the treatment of Native people in Alaska. People who had not experienced it would not be able to imagine the "intimidation, economic and otherwise, of the Natives and their friends . . ." in Alaska, he had said. Stevens had spoken for Native rights in his election campaign, and he agreed to work for Natives now without payment.

Stevens recommended that the Natives file appeals from the Alaska BLM office to BLM headquarters in Washington, D.C. It was important, he thought, to get a paper trail of the claims established. Both protests and new claims by Natives needed documentation, which meant taking oral testimony from villagers all across Alaska on their memories of traditional land use patterns. Soon BIA attorneys and Alaska Legal Service personnel fanned out across the state documenting Native land use. By 1965 Alaska Natives had filed hundreds of protests and new land claims. Because many of them overlapped, the total acreage exceeded the total land area in the state. It was chaos. There would be no economic development in Alaska on any disputed land until Native land claims were settled.

Henry Forbes could not fund the *Tundra Times* indefinitely and to raise funds the paper held a banquet, which became an annual event whose invitations were coveted. Interior Secretary Udall was the guest speaker at the banquet in 1966, and announced his intention to impose a moratorium on "the process of patenting state land selections in order to preserve status of Alaska lands until Native Claims can be settled."

*Gov. Walter Hickel,
development visionary.
(Courtesy Anchorage
Museum of History
and Art)*

Shortly afterward, in December 1966, the he cancelled an oil and gas lease sale scheduled for an area near Point Hope of the northwest Arctic coast. The following spring, he made good on his word, stopping leasing and "all other activity," including state land selections, on all federal public land in Alaska, in other words, a "land freeze." "All other activity" included state land selections, bringing to a halt one of the most important foundations of Alaska's future economic development, and a potent, tangible symbol of Alaskan independence. In December 1968, after Richard Nixon was elected President, Udall made the freeze permanent. He signed a public order withdrawing 262 million acres of land in Alaska, prohibiting its appropriation until the claims issue had been settled.

State officials and journalists reacted harshly. Many Alaskans felt betrayed. In February 1967, newly elected Governor Walter Hickel filed suit in federal court to overturn Udall's land freeze. The judge ruled for the state, that Native presence did not prevent the land from being "vacant, unappropriated and unreserved." The Ninth Circuit Court reversed the decision. The initial victory helped to assuage anger in the state, but not for long. In 1968 Alaska's congressional delegation arranged for hearings in Alaska on a bill to grant title to Alaska Natives to millions of acres of traditionally utilized land. Natives gathered from every part of the state to explain traditional use of the land by their own generation, and by their ancestors before them. One after another, old and young, they padded to the microphones in mukluks and moccasins to tell of hunting in river valleys and mountain bowls, of fishing in the same stream mouth since time immemorial, and of their cultural respect for the land. Almost all made a plea that their ancient land rights be honored so that their culture could be sustained. Collectively, it was the plaint of a frightened but defiant people.

Many Alaskans did not hear the plea or, if they did, considered Alaska's economic development a higher priority than Native rights. A spokesman for the Alaska Miners' Association, George Moerlein, argued that the Natives had no right to any land in Alaska, as Forester Frank Heintzleman had argued in 1947. Robert Atwood, editor of the *Anchorage Daily Times*, the state's largest-circulation newspaper and mouthpiece of the chambers of commerce, argued that Natives had no right to destroy the state's economic potential. To give Natives title to large areas of Alaska, Atwood argued, would send Alaska back to the Stone Age. As salmon industry spokesman W.C. Arnold had argued in 1946, Atwood suggested that if Alaska was to be set aside for Natives, the non-Natives may as well go back to the lower states, for Alaska's riches would remain undeveloped.

In January 1968, Governor Hickel convened a task force of Native leaders to draft a settlement bill acceptable to the Natives. Its membership included more than a dozen recognized leaders, and its chair, Willie Hensley, had just written a paper on the theory of aboriginal title for a graduate seminar at the University of Alaska taught by one of the state's leading jurists. The task force met for ten days after the Native hearings and introduced a few ideas for a settlement. Natives should be granted forty million acres of land, corresponding to traditionally utilized areas and $20 million for extinguishments of title to the rest of Alaska's land. Also, for ten years they should be paid 10 percent of the federal mineral lease revenue promised the state.

In the meantime, some similar ideas had come from a different quarter. On March 27, 1964, Alaska had suffered the strongest earthquake ever recorded in North America. Measured at 9.2 on the Richter scale, the quake lasted five minutes. One hundred thirty-one people died; property and infrastructure damage totaled $500 million. Several Native villages were destroyed. The resulting tsunami traveled across the Gulf of Alaska and down the Pacific Coast, killing several people in Oregon and California. President Johnson and the Congress responded with quick and substantial direct aid, and low-interest loans for rebuilding. Johnson appointed a blue-ribbon committee to coordinate the effort.

In 1965, soon after Secretary Udall implemented the land freeze, Senator Bartlett and Senator Henry M. Jackson of Washington State redirected the reconstruction committee to address the Native claims dilemma in Alaska. Renaming the group the Federal Field Committee for Development Planning in Alaska, Jackson called for a comprehensive survey of Alaska Native conditions, and a framework for solving the claims problem.

The committee produced its report in 1968, titled *Alaska Natives and the Land*. In the survey, researchers found that Alaska Natives collectively had the lowest living conditions of any group of people in the United States. They had the highest rates of infant mortality and communicable disease, the lowest cash income, the poorest housing and water and sewer facilities, the lowest educational attainment, and the lowest cash income, among other factors. The committee concluded that Alaska Natives were so poor in material amenities as to be denied equal opportunity. At a time when Americans were focusing on Martin Luther King's poor peoples' march on Washington, the committee's report had the effect of tearing the wraps off a family secret and exposing it to public scrutiny.

The Federal Field Committee also documented traditional land use for every Native place in Alaska. They found documented use of approximately forty million acres of land. With the statehood entitlement in mind, the committee made a recommendation regarding a claims settlement. The Natives should receive between four and seven million acres of land, and $100 million in compensation. They should also be paid 10 percent of the royalty revenue from federal mineral leases in Alaska for ten years. The similarity to the Native task force report reflected the Natives' involvement in the Field Committee's work.

But there was no further serious work on a claims settlement until 1969. By then several elements had changed the circumstances in which a settlement would be pursued. After his election in 1968, President Nixon had appointed Walter Hickel Secretary of the Interior. And when Bob Bartlett died of a heart attack in December 1968, Hickel, just before leaving office, had appointed Ted Stevens to assume the Senate seat.

Hickel was belligerent early in his confirmation process, asserting that what Secretary Udall could do with a pen, he, Hickel, could undo with a pen. The Native community was alarmed, and organized to stop Hickel's confirmation unless he promised to retain the freeze. Hickel's appointment was problematical for other reasons as well, and he eventually made the necessary promise, which the senate committee made a condition of his confirmation.

After Hickel's confirmation, oil lobbyists, Native leaders, and state and federal officials worked assiduously to produce a settlement. Issues included the amount of compensation and how it would be funded, and the amount of acreage to which Alaska Natives would gain title. The Interior Department pushed for only 12.5 million acres of land, and $500 million in compensation, but no royalty revenue. This was not helpful. The AFN accepted the $500 million, insisted on forty million acres, and wanted 2 percent of the mineral royalty in perpetuity. And the Native organization introduced a remarkable new idea: development stock companies. AFN leaders wanted a mechanism that would keep the money working for Alaska Natives forever. An individual cash payout would dissipate the money quickly. More importantly, they sought a way to maintain a communal connection among village and regional Native groups in the face of forces that increasingly were drawing people out of villages and away from traditional culture. Economic development corporations in which all Natives were stockholders seemed to be the answer. With the compensatory award invested for profit, a stock dividend could be paid to individual Native stockholders, and their heirs, as long as the corporation continued in existence. If the corporations held title to the land, Natives would at least have the option of remaining in their home villages, continuing a subsistence life style, supplemented by dividend income.

This was an extraordinary innovation. It represented highly creative and courageous thinking. It would preserve Native land and villages that lay in the path of the inexorable, dominating expansion of American economic development into the last frontier wilds of the country. The Native leadership decided to use a mode of thought alien to Native culture, capitalism, to protect the basis of Native culture, the land. That this innovation came from the Native leadership demonstrated their capability, their commitment to the future of Native culture and Native identity, and their increasing political power. The idea of the Native economic development corporation would become the central mechanism of the eventual claims settlement act.

There was another significant aspect of the AFN proposal. The 2 percent royalty, to be paid in perpetuity, represented substantive state participation in the Native claims settlement. In part, the state would be buying land from the Natives.

Once again, the state reacted harshly. Governor Keith Miller, who had replaced Hickel upon his appointment as Interior Secretary, rejected the idea of the state paying anything. The Natives had no right to state land, Miller wrote to Congress, and state land was any land the state wanted, up to its 104 million-acre entitlement. Agreeing, the *Anchorage Times* attacked attorneys from outside the state who were advising AFN (including former U.S. Supreme Court Justice Arthur Goldberg and former U.S. Attorney General Ramsey Clark.), implying they had duped the Natives. Alaska's economic growth and prosperity was at issue for Miller and *Times* editor Robert Atwood, and Native rights were subordinate. They based their assertion that state land selections should come first on the statehood act, which, they insisted, was a solemn compact that could not be altered without the state's prior approval. This notion defied American constitutional history, but that seemed not within Atwood's purview. Senator Stevens attempted to breathe some realism and some sensitivity to Native equality into the discussion, urging the governor and the Anchorage Chamber of Commerce to support a compromise, 2 percent of the royalty for a limited time. He feared and regretted, he said, a polarized Alaska with Natives pitted against non-Natives. But he made little headway at home.

Congress did not write the final bill that became the Alaska Native claims settlement until the summer of 1971. Historians Mary Berry and Peter Coates have separately reconstructed the story of the bill's final passage. Discussions on different bills encountered different challenges in each chamber, actually causing an impasse in the House. The oil companies provided the energy and focus that broke the deadlock and moved the process toward completion. Realizing that no pipeline could be built until Native claims were settled, lobbyists concentrated their efforts on getting the state to accept this reality. They were helped greatly by a change of administration in Alaska. In the 1970 election, former Democratic governor William Egan defeated Keith Miller. Egan had made clear in his campaign that if elected, he would cooperate with the federal government in seeking a compromise. The state's principal agent in this new stance was the man Egan chose as his attorney general, John E. Havelock. Spending considerable time in Washington, D.C., Havelock insisted that the state remain "flexible," which greatly aided the congressional delegation. In delicate negotiations he, Nick Begich, the state's lone congressman, and Senator Stevens established a common state position. When Native leaders came to agreement on two key elements, how land selection would proceed and how the money would be distributed, the act was essentially complete.

ANCSA was monumental, landmark legislation, perhaps the most generous settlement ever between the federal government and American

Natives. In a comprehensive manner probably not possible any other way, the grant of land and money to Alaska Natives collectively confirmed their equal legitimacy and stature in Alaska life, for those who needed it confirmed, which, given Alaska's racial climate, may have been many. Over the three decades following the act's passage, disparagement of Alaska Natives virtually disappeared from the press and from common discourse in the state, save among an inconsequential, extremist fringe. Perry Eaton, a Native CEO born in Kodiak and director of construction for a showpiece Native cultural center that opened in Anchorage in 2000, said in an interview "the place we enjoy as Alaska Natives today wouldn't exist without [the claims settlement act]. It gives us a tremendous amount of stature and control over our destiny, much greater than we had before." The act changed the way the people of Alaska view Natives, Eaton said.

> As people we were not taken seriously as a political force. In fact, much of the non-Native leadership was amused that indigenous people would come forward with the audacity to claim land. Today, thirty years later, there is a very honest respect for Native leadership.

This does not mean there is no longer a Native "problem" in Alaska, for major issues and challenges remain, and the persistent pursuit of a states' rights agenda by the legislature and other state leaders has tended to polarize relations between Natives and non-Natives in some areas. But race is no longer the context in which questions raised by the challenges are debated, at least not overtly. This can be considered a civil rights triumph. Then-Representative (now Senator) John Kyl said on the House floor when the act passed that body, "We recognize Alaska Natives' birthright with this bill." Today in Alaska that birthright is taken for granted. Today, the racial component in Alaska society is more complex, focused on the state's obligation to fund village education and to support the economic sustainability of Alaska Native villages.

In 1971 the claims settlement act granted fee simple title to Alaska Natives to forty million acres of land; the land was based around villages, and in traditionally utilized areas, as identified in the Federal Field Committee report. In compensation for extinguishment of title to Alaska's remaining 330 million acres, Natives were paid $925.5 million dollars, $425 million by Congressional appropriation over five years, and $500 million from the 2 percent federal mineral royalty paid to the state over twenty years. The money was paid to twelve regional development corporations (a thirteenth corporation made up of nonresident Alaska Natives was authorized and later formed in Seattle) and as many village development corporations as wished to form of the 211 recognized in the act. The capitalization was split between the regional (at large) and village corporations within each region, and all Alaska Natives (one-quarter blood quantum) enrolled as members of one of these corporations. The for-profit corporations were chartered under the laws of incorporation of the State of Alaska.

Though the corporations needed time to organize and become viable, today most are financially successful, partly due to an opportunity to sell tax losses in the 1990s, and several have begun to pay substantial dividends to their stockholders. Many have real estate and operating company holdings across America. Profiles and financial data are available for each on the worldwide web. Though there is more to the history of Native/non-Native relations in Alaska, which we will examine further on, the claims settlement act represents a milestone. In the context of civil rights, the 1971 act came at precisely the right time, nearly coincident with the height of the civil rights movement, soon after the assassinations of Martin Luther King, Jr., and Robert F. Kennedy, and just as the American Indian Movement and less radical Indian protest drew Americans' attention to the issue of Indian equality.

5

"Big Oil," ANCSA, and the Transformation

ʖ ʗ

The Alaska Native Claims Settlement Act became the context for economic and political development in Alaska after the discovery of the massive oil deposit at Prudhoe Bay in 1967. Without ANCSA, there would have been no pipeline, no oil production, no oil. The oil pipeline had to cross Alaska, and that meant crossing Native-claimed land; development of the deposit would not happen until the Native claims had been settled. Virtually every aspect of Alaska's history since 1971 has been framed and influenced by the act. There are three reasons for this. First, the state's economy and the administration of state government are uniquely dependent on tax revenue generated from oil production. Eighty-five percent of general fund revenue is generated from oil taxation, either directly or through investment. Approximately 43 percent of the entire economy is based on oil revenue and the Alaska Permanent Fund dividend. In Anchorage, Fairbanks, Kenai, and Valdez, the oil industry provides the largest private sector payroll. In the Matanuska Valley, oil generates more jobs than any other industry. In 1999, the oil industry spent more than $2.1 billion in Alaska. Of that, $422 million was in direct payroll; another $1.7 billion was spent on drilling, construction, supplies, and services. A research study estimated the industry generated 33,573 jobs statewide from its in-state expenditures, 20 percent of the private sector payroll. At the same time, 35 percent of the total economy is federal spending. Alaska receives the highest level of federal funds per capita of any state. For direct state revenue, there are few economic alternatives to oil taxation, although tourism, aviation, mining, and the forest products industry do contribute to the economy. But economies of scale and global market conditions prohibit manufacturing, inhibit agriculture, and militate against much diversification of the economy.

Second, by bringing the civil rights revolution effectively into the state, ANCSA generated much greater social, political, and economic racial equity. While issues remain, the thirty thousand Alaska Natives, 30 percent of the Native population, who live in urban Alaska are for the most part racially invisible. They are well integrated into the society, their leaders serve in the highest echelons of politics and public service bodies, and Native corporate executives are as familiar at business and policy gatherings as any other category of person.

The third aspect of the claim settlement's impact on modern Alaska will be the focal point of the remainder of this study: the act's environmental provisions. These included authorization for the Secretary of the Interior to withdraw 80 million acres of Alaska in new federal conservation units, subject to Congress's approval by December 17, 1978, and mandated appointment of a joint federal/state land use planning commission to make recommendations on federal and state land disposition. When finally completed, in the Alaska National Interest Lands Conservation Act (ANILCA) of 1980, the new conservation selections would be the most significant environmental legislation in American history.

It might be surprising that ANCSA dealt with the Alaska environment until one remembers that its proximate purpose was to clear the way for economic development: construction of the Alaska oil pipeline. But, as we have seen, raised environmental consciousness in the United States drew attention to Alaska even before the discovery of oil at Prudhoe Bay. This was a consequence of the statehood campaign. The chief theme of the campaign was that statehood would "open" Alaska, whose development had been thwarted by laggard and insensitive federal policies. Conservation groups across the country understood the implications of "opening" Alaska; it meant commodifying the "last wilderness." The conservation group in Alaska opposed to the creation of ANWR in 1959 and 1960 made that unmistakably clear.

In 1963 the national Wilderness Society held its annual meeting in Alaska, at Camp Denali outside the boundary of Mt. McKinley National Park. The purpose was to raise awareness of Alaska conservation issues for national environmental organizations. Delegates produced a statement calling on state and federal officials to make provisions for the preservation of wilderness areas in land use planning for Alaska. Alaskans were resistant to the idea, but one group took heed: the Federal Field Committee. The Committee understood its charge to be to find a framework not only for settling Native claims, but for planning all land distribution in Alaska. As a result, while their recommendation on title and money for Natives were much more favorable to the state than to Natives, their reports did call for land planning in Alaska, including identifying areas which had merit as conservation units. To identify these lands, the Committee consulted, among others, the Wilderness Society; the state was unresponsive to Committee requests for joint planning.

Realizing that congressional action would be the only way to protect any wilderness in Alaska, in early 1971 a dozen national conservation groups,★ calling themselves the Alaska Coalition, organized to lobby in Washington to include conservation withdrawals in the claims bill. That so many groups existed, and were willing to pool their resources to address Alaska environmental issues, suggested the significance of Alaska land to the American people at the time, and the depth of feeling among environmental activists. The Alaska Coalition, which would change its name to the Alaska Public Interest Coalition (APIC) later in the year, became the primary lobbying group on several Alaska environmental issues. Headed by the Sierra Club's executive director, Chuck Clusen, it became the largest and most powerful citizen conservation organization in American history and made battlegrounds of three Alaska issues over the next two decades: the Alaska pipeline construction project, the Alaska lands act, and logging and development in the Tongass National Forest. Its membership grew at one time to ten million people.

In 1971, APIC lobbied Congress to include in ANCSA a five-year moratorium on land selections after passage of the act for the purpose of land planning in Alaska, specifically, to identify "national interest" lands there; their proposal included establishing a planning commission to designate land categories and uses across the state. The criteria for designation included the concept of ecosystem, identifying interrelated systems of flora and fauna that manifested a fundamental integrity, a unity borne of dependence. But for a number of APIC members, these were details. In truth, many in the environmental lobby hoped to stop

---

★The groups included the Wilderness Society, the Sierra Club, National Wildlife Federation, the Wildlife Management Institute, Friends of the Earth, Defenders of Wildlife, Trout Unlimited, the National Rifle Association, Zero Population Growth, Environmental Action, Citizens' Committee on Natural Resources, and the Alaska Action Committee. They called themselves the Alaska Coalition.

the pipeline. To these advocates, the idea of wilderness, manifest in Alaska's countless mountain peaks and river valleys, its Arctic tundra, and its great forests, was more important than the 20 percent of American oil consumption that the Prudhoe Bay field would contribute. Oil, they argued, was ephemeral; wilderness was forever, until sullied by human imprint, particularly that of our modern economy, industrial capitalism. The nation, they believed, had a greater interest in wilderness lands in Alaska than in Alaska's oil.

Of course, for many Alaskans, "Alaska" and "national interest lands" when used together represented a contradiction in terms. One small group of extremists in Alaska urged secession rather than allowing the federal government any comment on Alaska land disposal. But others saw a value in long-range planning; it would eliminate ambiguity and uncertainty, and therefore actually encourage development. Leaders in the state legislature took this view, and passed a resolution supporting the idea, and in Washington, D.C., Alaska's junior senator, Mike Gravel, introduced the idea for inclusion in the claims act, proposing creation of a five-year joint federal-state land use planning commission. The environmental provisions of the claims act and ultimately, the Alaska lands act, had their origins in Gravel's proposal.

In truth, it had taken more than thoughtful entreaties by those who believed in long-range planning to direct Gravel's attention, and that of the Alaska legislature, from the idea of conservation withdrawals. It had taken high drama. Over the winter of 1968-69, before he left for Washington to become Interior Secretary, Governor Hickel had authorized construction of a haul road from Fairbanks to Prudhoe Bay to move supplies north in anticipation of construction of the pipeline. Ignoring lessons other contractors had learned about road construction over permafrost, the contractor simply bulldozed away the protective vegetation. In summer the road melted into the permafrost and became a water-filled ditch. The project was an environmental disaster, a permanent, 390-mile scar across the mountains and the tundra, impossible to remove. For some, this was the beginning of the despoliation of the wilderness they had predicted. Alaska was being "opened," its wilderness befouled, cut in half by the imprint of man, an imprint that was apparently indelible.

In March 1970, as now-Secretary Hickel prepared to issue permits for a new road along the proposed pipeline right-of-way, preparations for construction, and perhaps the pipeline project itself, were summarily halted. Three environmental groups, the Wilderness Society, Friends of the Earth, and the Environmental Defense Fund, filed suit in federal court to stop its construction. The suit charged that plans submitted by the entity created to construct the line, TAPS, the Trans-Alaska Pipeline System, violated the new National Environmental Policy Act (NEPA) and the 1920 Mineral Leasing Act. Primarily, the conservationists charged, the oil companies had not done the scientific and engineering studies needed, and had no idea how to build a pipeline in permafrost so as to mitigate environmental impact. A federal judge reviewed the plans and agreed; he issued an injunction halting any construction activity.

When they realized the implications, Alaskans were aghast. Environmentalists made two arguments. First, proper studies needed to be done and a sound engineering plan developed. That could take months, perhaps more. Second, some critics believed there should be no pipeline at all, under any circumstances. They hoped to keep Alaska wilderness untrammeled. If this group prevailed, Alaska's future would be fundamentally altered and the dreams of socioeconomic advance held by so many would go wanting. In addition, just prior to the environmental suit, five Native villages on the Yukon River filed their own suit, charging that TAPS had promised training and jobs for the Natives, but had taken no steps to implement their commitment.

The Natives' suit was resolved swiftly—the oil companies guaranteed Native job training and jobs—though not before the airing of much ugly anti-Native rhetoric. But the environmental suit would last three years. As it dragged on, it generated an accumulating fear. Some worried that perhaps the critics were correct; a pipeline could not be built in permafrost. Perhaps environmentalism was a stronger, more permanent force than people had thought. The implications struck at the heart of modern culture in Alaska. Alaskans recognized that the material well-being they demanded could not be realized without the kind of investment represented by oil production and the money it would bring to Alaska. And now the new national environmental consciousness, manifest in NEPA and, for those who remembered, the 1964 Wilderness Act, threatened to steal away the promise of riches.

From the time of the battle over Hetch Hetchy valley in the California Mountains between 1907 and 1913, conservation struggles over public lands have been fought on a national scale. Invariably outnumbered in their own states, conservationists have appealed to a national audience, hoping commitment to ideal preservation of unique or dwindling resources will generate sufficient political pressure to restrain the forces of development and convictions of the legitimacy of resource utilization.

In other words, advocates of preservation have hoped to use the sentiments of people outside the region they wish to preserve to impose restrictions on the people within that region. The tactic can only succeed if the advocates can generate sufficient publicity to place the issue before the general public, and if they can bring the public's support to bear on those who must make the land use decision. This tactic failed in Hetch Hetchy in 1913, but it succeeded increasingly in the 1950s and 1960s, most particularly in 1956, when environmental groups stopped Congress from approving construction of a high dam at Echo Park in Dinosaur National Monument on the Colorado River. Many analysts have viewed the Echo Park battle as the beginning of modern environmentalism.

Local people affected by national preservation campaigns are likely to feel victimized. Self-governance is one of the cardinal principles of American political ideology; the country was born in a revolution founded on that principle. Thus, local people are likely to resent outside influences. They will feel that the decision over resource use, or any other public responsibility, should be theirs, even if they decision they might make should be the same that might be made by outsiders. Conservation decisions made by Congress in response to national environmental campaigns, endorsed and supported by people who have no direct economic stake in the consequences, and who may not even know the location of the land in question, are painful for local communities affected. That pain is often exacerbated because the locals feel that the decisions manifest and impose ideologies contradictory to their own, viz., the superiority of national will and policy over state and local policy, and the dominance of wilderness held in *situ,* rather than developed so as to serve the demands of personal profit and community expansion. Most Alaskans felt such pain acutely during the fight over the Alaska pipeline, and subsequently, the struggles over the Alaska lands bill and the Tongass National Forest.

But while the Alaskan press and state government officials railed at the court, the oil industry did not wait for an outcome. Company executives directed industry engineers to produce the kinds of studies necessary, and to redesign the project. They completed the work during 1972, submitting the final plans to the Council on Environmental Quality, established by NEPA. In March that year CEQ issued its environmental impact statement, an engineering and environmental tome of nine volumes. The CEQ approved the project.

Alaskans breathed a sigh of relief as the federal court lifted the injunction. But the relief was short lived, for the plaintiffs immediately appealed. In February 1973, the appeals court handed the controversy off to Congress. Basing its decision on legislation going back to the Mineral Leasing Act of 1920, the court ruled that only Congress had the authority to resolve outstanding issues dealing with the pipeline right-of-way. There the matter rested through the spring and summer of 1973.

In Alaska, pessimism reigned. Senator Gravel formed a new group, modeled on the organizations that had fought the statehood campaign, to try to mobilize national support for the Alaska project. The state legislature appropriated money to support it. But the Alaskans found interest around the country modest at best. Expanding the parameters of concern for environmental impact, Congress that year passed the Endangered Species Act, placing the value and integrity of nature above the interest of economic development when the two should come into conflict. Environmental consciousness was at its highest peak in American history. People across the nation were not moved by arguments about the economic impact of cancellation of the pipeline project on Alaska. Gravel told the newspaper in Fairbanks that "if a national referendum were to be held on the Trans-Alaska Pipeline it would probably be defeated." Members of the Pioneers of Alaska, a social and service club of long-time residents, talked of suing the national Sierra Club for a billion dollars if the pipeline was not built.

In Washington, D.C., the Senate began hearings on a bill to authorize construction of the pipeline. Opposition was formidable, for environmental groups saw the bill as a test of NEPA. That act had been conceived for just such projects. At the hearings critics repeated the charge from the environmental suit, and threatened to take the issue back to court if Congress passed the bill. When the bill came to the Senate floor in July, Senator Gravel proposed an amendment prohibiting further court action on the environmental issues of the pipeline. The vote on the Gravel amendment would be the critical vote on pipeline authorization. Even supporters of the project recognized that precluding court action on such a massive project would set the worst kind of example regarding environmental protection, and opposed the amendment. But in a climactic vote, the Senate tied 49-49 on the issue, and Vice-president Spiro Agnew cast the deciding vote in favor of the amendment.

The pipeline still might not have been authorized. But in October, the United States stepped in to aid Israel in a new Arab-Israeli war. In retaliation, the Arab states in OPEC imposed an oil embargo on the U.S. Suddenly, Americans did not have enough gasoline, and as block-long lines formed at service stations and citizens found they could purchase petrol only on alternate days and in rationed amounts, Alaskan oil achieved a new popularity with the American public. President Nixon called on Congress to pass the authorization bill, and in November, both houses did, by overwhelming majorities. For Alaska, the crisis was over.

By this time, the industry had heard the message of the American people that the pipeline needed to be constructed and operated in an environmentally respectful manner. Waiving of NEPA in the authorization act did not mean disregard of the landscape, particularly the long-term impacts. The project would go forward with assiduous monitoring of its effects by federal and state officials. Construction of the line would take three years, and the process fulfilled all of the prophesied superlatives. Over twenty-eight thousand personnel worked on various aspects of the project, which cost $7.7 billion, vastly beyond the industry's 1970 estimate of $900,000. Money flowed easily. The industry determined to complete the project in record time, and did, but at great cost. The separate company created by the leaseholders to build and operate the line, Alyeska Pipeline Service Company, had to pay high wages and provide the best food and accommodations and other amenities to maintain the labor force. The high wages resulted in typical boomtown conditions in Fairbanks and Anchorage. Off-duty workers spent lavishly in the two cities, where crime rates rose substantially and unemployment dropped to near zero. A number of gangland-style murders were associated with the Teamsters Union in Fairbanks, which controlled much of the labor and supply for the project. At one point the union was banking $1 million a week in dues. The boomtown atmosphere intimidated local residents who learned firsthand the nature of the raucous frontier they celebrated in tales of the gold rush.

As advocates had insisted it would, the pipeline trod lightly on the landscape. There were incidents of stream pollution and needless inundation of the forest and tundra. But these were few, and quickly corrected. The impact on the notion of wilderness was more substantial. It was no longer possible to think of the unspoiled Arctic. There might be countless miles of undeveloped land, of snow and caribou and Arctic fox, land with a few Eskimo villages whose hunters still took seal in the winter and conducted a spring whale hunt. But the land had definitely been permanently altered. Many Alaskans did not understand the environmental plaint about lost wilderness. The imprint of the line on the landscape was barely perceptible, they insisted. The total land area taken by the right-of-way was sixty square miles, a tiny fraction of Alaska land. Historian Peter Coates reported an incident in which Vide Bartlett, the widow of former Senator Bob Bartlett, attempted to explain this to a group of environmentalists whom she had invited to her Anchorage home. She covered all of her living and dining room carpet with newsprint from the Sunday paper. Then she stretched a thin black thread across it. That was as much environment as the pipeline would take up, she said, an area nearly unnoticeable. But the environmentalists explained in anguish that Mrs. Bartlett had missed the point. Once a pipeline was stitched across the landscape, it could no longer be called wilderness. Robert Marshall's dream of a pristine Arctic wilderness was gone.

Alaska oil began to flow through the pipeline from Prudhoe Bay to Valdez on June 20, 1977. The first tanker departed the Valdez terminal on August 1.

$$\bowtie \bowtie$$

Alaskans' euphoria over impending riches was somewhat muted by continuing discussion of Congress's intention to withdraw millions of acres in Alaska for inclusion in new federal conservation units, as provided in ANCSA. Once Congress approved ANCSA, state and federal officials and Natives found they had much work to do while they awaited the outcome of the environmental suits to stop the pipeline. The Secretary was given ninety days to select 80 million acres in new federal conservation units, subject to Congress's approval by December 1978. After the ninety days, the state would be able to select the 77 million acres remaining from its statehood act entitlement, again, provisionally. But the act was not clear on this process, particularly on the question of whether the federal selections could be made in areas the state wished to select. In addition, the act mandated the appointment of the joint federal/state land use planning commission, which was to make recommendations on state and federal selections. There was considerable confusion.

Recognizing the significance of the Secretary's selections for the future of Alaska wilderness, APIC purchased $30,000 worth of newspaper space across the nation asking people to write the Secretary (the ads included a coupon) to urge him to select all 80 million acres, and more. The campaign was hugely successful, and in March 1972, Secretary Rogers C. B. Morton withdrew the 80 million acres in areas the conservation lobby and officials in several federal agencies had recommended. He also set aside 45 million acres for study for possible inclusion in future conservation units, withdrew 40 million acres around villages and in traditionally used areas for Native selection, and set aside an additional 3 million from which Natives could select "in lieu" or make–up lands should any of the conservation withdrawals take traditional Native lands. Finally, the Secretary designated 35 million acres for state selection; further state selections would have to wait until the conservation and Native selections were complete. In all, it was an extraordinary action that surprised most people. It was more than the conservationists had hoped for, consistent with the act's mandate for Natives, and seemed to freeze the Alaskans out of the process.

In Alaska, there was anger. Congressman Nick Begich called it a "massive land grab." Attorney General Havelock called it a "sell out of the people of Alaska." The *Anchorage Times* said it was a "dirty deed." Soon afterward, the state filed a suit challenging the withdrawals. In the meantime, the planning commission began its work, taking testimony from all parties, and in August recommended resolution of a number of federal/state conflicts. Federal and state negotiators also worked independently of the commission, and in September the state withdrew its lawsuit in exchange for the right to make some immediate selections in areas slated for conservation. Then, in December 1973, the Secretary forwarded his final recommendation for conservation withdrawals to the Congress; they totaled over 83 million acres. The state was somewhat mollified, for even though officials had not been permitted to select all the lands they wished, the Secretary had left available most of the lands the state wanted. Conservationists were not pleased, for they had hoped for considerably more acreage, and they wanted much of the withdrawn land classified as wilderness. The battle over Alaska lands was far from over, and its more virulent confrontations were yet to come.

In the face of the Watergate drama of 1973-74, the Alaska lands bill slipped from congressional attention. But Jimmy Carter made conservation in Alaska a major campaign initiative, and when he was elected in 1976 signaled that he expected Congress to act before its self-imposed deadline expired in 1978. Congress had passed the National Forest Management Act and the Federal Land Policy and Management Act in 1976, both of which mandated public planning processes and citizen involvement in the management of federal public lands. National environmental sentiment still ran high, and the environmental lobby pressured sympathetic members of Congress to take an aggressive stance on Alaska lands.

On the first day of the new Congress in 1977, Representative Morris Udall of Arizona, younger brother of former Secretary Stewart Udall, introduced a bill calling for 115 million acres of Alaska conservation reserves, nearly half again more acreage than provided in ANCSA. The bill was designated H.R. 39, and would become infamous in Alaska by that name. The bill would protect the environmental "crown jewels of Alaska," Udall said, a phrase that would be heard often in the course of the debate; the crown jewels were Alaska's "most spectacular natural environments, recreation areas, and wildlife habitats." The bill would create ten new national parks and expand existing ones, create fourteen new wildlife refuges and twenty-three wild and scenic rivers, and enlarge the two national forests. About two-thirds of known mineral deposits were left out of the proposed conservation units. Half of the acreage within them would be designated as wilderness, more than doubling the national wilderness system created by the 1964 Wilderness Act. The bill was truly monumental.

The House assigned the bill to a subcommittee for General Oversight and Alaska Lands, chaired by John Seiberling of Ohio. The subcommittee held hearings in the spring and summer of 1977, in five cities in the "lower 48" states and a score of communities in Alaska. In each of the stateside cities, the Alaska Coalition publicized the hearings widely before the congressmen arrived. As a result, over two thousand people testified, almost all of them speaking for the bill. The bill proposed that Natives would continue to have access to traditional resources within conservation units. One hunter from the village of Minto told the congressmen that if their generation failed to protect the land, God might forgive them, but their children would not. The Alaska chapters of the national environmental groups felt beleaguered but buoyed by the testimony at successive sites. Urban Alaska might be determined to keep Alaska open for development, but village Alaska sought protection.

The *New York Times* called local opposition "vociferously hostile." The *Anchorage Times* decried "locking up" the mineral resources of Alaska, making the riches of the national parks accessible only to "butterfly chasers" and backpackers. Alaska was "pioneering country," former Governor Hickel told a *New York Times* reporter. "We're saying to the Government," Hickel said, "you've screwed up enough of our lives. You come up here two weeks a year and tell us how to live but you won't come up here and live and make it work." A member of the state House of Representatives called Udall's bill "the most colonialist attitude about a sovereign state I have ever seen." Former Attorney General Edgar Paul Boyko wrote that

> *The perennial hunger of Alaskans for land . . . has, it seems, been forever thwarted by Federal and state bureaucrats using various devices, such as withdrawals, reservations, national forests, national parks, wilderness areas, special uses, classifications, planning studies, holding categories, land freezes, etc., ad infinitum and ad nauseum, to keep the values of land artificially high and to prevent the inhabitants of America's largest state from acquiring land to any degree approaching their needs.*

Tom Snapp, editor of a Fairbanks weekly paper, wrote, "We were supposed to be taken in as a state on an equal basis, but we're not going to be allowed to develop the way other states develop their resources."

> *We're going to be nipped in the bud just as Fairbanks is becoming a commercial and communications center. It's reneging on the promises of statehood, and I don't believe the people would have voted statehood if they had known this was going to happen.*

The conviction that Alaska was a "frontier society" that could generate its own economic well-being if left to its own devices lay at the heart of much of the criticism of the Udall "lock up." Whether Alaska leaders truly believed that is difficult to determine. Judging from the antagonism of daily news reports and editorials, it is likely that many of the residents did. Hickel believed that the resources of Alaska should belong to Alaskans to use for their own aggrandizement. To develop Alaska meant to extract the resources as the base of an economy that could expand, providing jobs, livelihoods, and material comfort for all who wanted to live in the state. He could not understand why that opportunity for development should be stopped. The idea that the land should not be developed, should not fill up with people, should be left intact, struck him as ludicrous, just as Gifford Pinchot had thought it ludicrous that a tree should die in the forest, unused, uncut, uncommodified. But this was precisely the agenda of the environmentalists, and they enjoyed the support of a majority of the population in the late 1970s, a fact many Alaskans could neither fathom nor accept.

But the Alaska Coalition took nothing for granted. Comprising in 1977-78 seventeen different environmental groups, the lobbyists made an all-out effort on the Alaska lands fight. Not only did Alaska represent

America's last wilderness, but also several recent significant challenges had shaken national confidence in environmentalism. That year, the Environmental Defense Fund had launched a suit on behalf of the snail darter, an obscure, small and noneconomic fish threatened with extinction by the planned construction of the Tellico Dam on the Tennessee River. The idea of species preservation clashed head-on with issues most Americans considered more important: flood control and irrigation. At the same time, research had begun on the habitat of the Northern Spotted Owl. Scientists were beginning to piece together information demonstrating the critical nature of old growth forest for the species' survival, information that would have a dramatic affect on the forest products industry. Recognizing a potential weakening of support, environmental groups meant to use Alaska lands to strengthen national commitment to ecological issues, and politically, to broaden their own political base and membership. At the same time, Alaskans committed to development benefited from increasing international competition for minerals, gas, and oil. Alaska had 60 percent of the nation's mineral wealth, Hickel asserted, and the nation's economic development would be stunted if the conservationists were allowed to wall it off by declaring it official wilderness. In one of the classic malapropisms of Alaska history, Hickel insisted, "We can't just let nature run wild!"

But the tide seemed to be running with the environmentalists' drive for a strong conservation bill for Alaska. As passed by the House, H.R. 39 would have set aside 122 million acres in new conservation units in Alaska, including 65 million designated as wilderness. The final vote on the bill was 279-31. Supporters hoped the overwhelming majority would put pressure on the Senate to accept the bill. But that did not happen. The Senate traditionally has been reluctant to pass any bill that significantly impacts a particular state over the strong objections of the senators from that state. This gave Alaska Senators Stevens and Gravel leverage, and instead of taking up the House bill, they persuaded the Senate to mark up its own bill. Stevens guided the process even though he was not on the appropriate committee. His tactic was to use every opportunity to delay the bill past the self-imposed deadline, December 1978. But he was a political realist, and recognized that compromise was probably necessary. If Congress did not produce a bill, Alaska would be left in limbo; every new resource project would be contested by the environmental lobby, with Alaska's future left at the mercy of piecemeal, and probably contradictory, federal court decisions. Senator Gravel, on

*Sen. Ted Stevens
and Eskimo leader
Willie Hensley at a
Fairbanks winter
festival.
(Courtesy
Anchorage Museum
of History and Art)*

the other hand, had said from the beginning of the 95th Congress that he would filibuster and kill any bill he did not like.

Gravel would be true to his word. As the Senate diddled over its Alaska bill through late summer and into the fall, environmentalists became increasingly concerned. Some began to think that Stevens and Gravel would be able to sidetrack the whole process, and six years of work would go for naught. One who thought so was Carter's Interior Secretary Cecil Andrus, former governor of Idaho. Principals on each side of the issue had met several times to try to work out a compromise, and had included the Secretary in their discussions. They had come very close. But Gravel had imposed last-minute demands that the others could not accept. These included mandated access corridors across the conservation units to guarantee potential development of nonselected or state-selected lands; a hydroelectric dam on the Susitna River near Anchorage; a clause prohibiting further conservation withdrawals in

Alaska; prohibition of the president's use of the Antiquities Act to temporarily withdraw land; and $800 million for access roads and recreational development. When the negotiations collapsed as a result, Andrus made it clear that he would use the Antiquities Act and any other means at his disposal to withdraw all the lands under discussion if Congress failed to produce legislation.

Others had thought of the Antiquities Act, also. More than one hundred members of Congress sent a letter to President Carter encouraging him to withdraw the lands by executive order if Congress failed to act. So did the Alaska Coalition. As the deadline drew nearer, Andrus took his threat public. The Alaska press was quick to notice. So was the AFN, whose president, Byron Mallott, contacted Andrus to ask about Native access in case the Secretary did withdraw lands. Andrus assured Mallott that he did intend to use the Antiquities Act, if necessary, and that allowances would be made for Native subsistence access if he did so. Meanwhile, in Washington, in the last hours of the 95th Congress, Gravel took to the Senate floor to filibuster a joint resolution to extend the deadline for two years. On October 14, the session expired with no Alaska bill.

State government officials in Alaska did not wait for the Secretary. Having provisional approval of 26 million acres, and the promise of an additional 35 million agreed upon by the land use planning commission and congressional negotiators, the state still had 43 million acres to complete its entitlement under the statehood act. State leaders had watched apprehensively as the Congress wrestled with the size and location of the proposed Alaska units, wondering what would be left when they were through. Andrus understood there was agreement that the state would wait until Congress passed an Alaska act before moving ahead on the last round of selections. But the state didn't wait. In early November, the state filed an application with the BLM for 41 million acres. Nearly one-quarter of the selections were in proposed new conservation units.

Now Andrus did not wait. Two days later he withdrew nearly 111 million acres of Alaska land, using the authority of the Federal Land Policy and Management Act of 1976. Andrus designated 40 million acres of the withdrawn land as study areas, thereby preventing mineral or other commercial activity, and at the request of the Agriculture Secretary, President Carter suspended the operation of public land laws on 11 million acres of the existing Tongass National Forest. Then, two weeks later, President Carter withdrew 56 million additional acres in Alaska, using the authority of the 1906 Antiquities Act, placing the land in seventeen new national monuments. This brought the total Carter administration withdrawals to 154 million; they were to last three years. This was unquestionably the most dramatic and sweeping withdrawal of public lands in the history of the nation, and it left Alaskans in disarray.

"Shocked State Leaders Try to Fathom Effect of Freeze," the *Fairbanks News Miner* told its readers. "Leaders React Angrily to Andrus' Withdrawals," the *Anchorage Times* proclaimed. Moderate Republican Governor Jay Hammond said, "It appears Alaska's worst fears have been realized." Some of the land was closed to sport hunting, Hammond said, which was "absolutely unacceptable." Gravel said, "I think it is clear the administration has overstepped the bounds of law," and the state attorney general announced an immediate suit to overturn the executive actions. Charles Clusen, executive director of the Alaska Coalition noted, "President Carter has now replaced Teddy Roosevelt as the greatest conservation president of all time." But Congressman Don Young complained that "Alaskans have been slanderously portrayed as land rapists by the preservation lobby and the President has chosen to believe this image." At a rally in Fairbanks, citizens burned Carter in effigy. The state legislature debated, but ultimately did not adopt, a measure to pay for legal assistance for people who might violate new monument boundaries, and a group living near Mt. McKinley organized a group snow machine trek into the extended boundaries of the national park there which they styled the "Great Denali Trespass." Park officials wisely did not interfere. Perhaps the most threatening action occurred in the non-Native village of Eagle on the Yukon River, which John McPhee had written about in his then-best selling book, *Coming into the Country*. The town council adopted a resolution saying, "We do not intend to obey the directives and regulations of the National Park Service." They did not advocate violence, the council said, but they could not be responsible for the actions of individual citizens. When the new director of the NPS Area Office appeared in the village in January 1979, he was confronted with signs saying, "National Park Service employees and anyone else advocating a dictatorship (including those locally who support National Park Service activities under the Antiquities Act) are not welcome here!"

The actions by Carter and Andrus had the effect intended; they produced an Alaska lands act before the end of the next Congress, but not quite in the way they had hoped. Environmentalists felt they had won the battle, and were in no mood to compromise. At the beginning of the 96th Congress, Morris Udall again introduced H.R. 39. But this version was a stronger environmental bill than the original, with many compromises eliminated. The environmental lobby reorganized to keep the pressure on Congress. But a new factor had entered the lists. In Alaska, a new lobby had formed during the 1977 hearings. Called Citizens for the Management of Alaska Lands (CMAL), the group included representatives from such groups as the Alaska Miners' Association, the Alaska Loggers' Association, and the Teamsters' Union. Leadership came as well from Alaska Lumber and Pulp Company, the Sitka pulp mill, and a strong minority group from Alaska's Native community. The first president of CMAL was Carl Marrs, an Aleut from the town of Seldovia on the Kenai Peninsula. The oil industry contributed significant funds, allowing CMAL to hire Langhorne "Tony" Motley, a talented attorney, Republican Party activist, and state commerce commissioner, as their Washington, D.C., lobbyist. Both the National Rifle Association and Exxon Corporation assigned their regular lobbyists in Washington to help, and the Alaska legislature contributed $2.5 million "to insure the interests of the State of Alaska are met."

Many in CMAL thought the legislation would mean the end of mining in Alaska, and the Alaska Miners' Association (AMA) took the lead in organizing the private lobbying effort. AMA held its first statewide convention in 1976, just as Udall and APIC were drafting H.R. 39. The miners invited a number of conservation organization leaders to address them on the place of mining in Alaska's future. Jack Hession, executive director of the Alaska chapter of the Sierra Club, used the opportunity to "deliver mining's eulogy." Confident that H.R. 39 would pass with prohibitions of mining in the conservation units, Hession assured the convention that most mineral resources in Alaska would not be affected. But, he said, environmentalism had proceeded so far that mining on federal conservation lands would be unacceptable to the American people. Hession's assurances were a wake-up call not just for the miners, but for all the interest groups that joined CMAL. Charles Hawley, executive director of the AMA, was one of the few who did understand just how dramatic the effect of ANCSA's conservation provisions might be, but he knew, too, that the miners alone would be ineffective in opposing Udall's bill. Hawley insisted that the miners were not against conservation, but "were aware of the danger of ill-conceived withdrawals of public lands." Ill-conceived, to the miners, meant new federal law that would eliminate mining activity in any part of Alaska where it was then being conducted, and where there were known mineral deposits. For loggers, it meant any part of the Tongass National Forest with "harvestable timber."

For the Teamsters it meant anything that might curtail Alaska's economic growth. "Something had to be done," Hawley wrote later. Accordingly, CMAL dedicated its efforts to reducing the wilderness imprint on Alaska to as small an area as politically possible. Though the Miners' Association started CMAL, the AMA represented a minority view among the Alaska development lobby, accepting the notion that there were areas of Alaska that needed protection.

But their position on withdrawals was not extreme. By contrast, Robert Weeden, a University of Alaska biologist who served as an environmental advisor in Governor Hammond's administration, argued that Alaska's population should be stabilized at about five hundred thousand. He thought that only "primitive" uses of the environment should be allowed, to sustain an alternative lifestyle, one characterized by subsistence harvest, minimum use of forest and water resources, and limited urban development. Weeden's model was Robert Marshall. He accepted Marshall's assertion that the people of Wiseman, a mixed, integrated community with whom Marshall had lived for over a year, were the "happiest people on earth." Freed of inflated material appetites, challenged by living daily in the wilderness, able to provide their subsistence, they could realize their potentials as human beings, and to live more honestly with one another and with nature. This was what Alaska could be, Weeden suggested. Governor Hammond met Weeden halfway. He pushed hard for a cooperative management model, in which the federal and state governments, Natives, and private developers would manage Alaska's resources and development together, instead of as mutually exclusive jurisdictional enclaves. A long-time wilderness guide, Hammond had opposed statehood because he feared galloping population increases and wholesale resource exploitation. Modest development and limited impact on the land were key ideas in Hammond's vision of Alaska's future.

But this was not the Alaska most of the state's residents wanted; and it was not the Alaska envisioned by CMAL. Governor Hammond, CMAL, and legislative leaders drew up a seven-point agenda that they would pursue exclusively and aggressively. It included title to all land selected by the state, including the 41 million acres selected in November 1978; state management of fish and wildlife; exclusion of viable resources from the conservation units; guaranteed access across conservation units; a clause prohibiting any further executive order withdrawals; guarantees for continuation of "traditional Alaskan lifestyles"; revocation of all 1978 Carter administration actions, i.e., the FLPMA and Antiquities Act withdrawals. With this agreement on the issues, and concerted, continuing effort, the Alaska lobby was very effective. Nonetheless, the Alaska Coalition was able to hold most supporters in line, and in the summer of 1979 the House passed the new, more conservationist version of H.R. 39 by a vote of 360-65. Again, environmentalists were hopeful that the lopsided nature of the vote would spur the Senate to action, and again they were disappointed. The Senate would not take up an Alaska lands bill until the summer of 1980. In the meantime, Secretary Andrus changed the classification of 40 million withdrawn acres in Alaska from three-year to twenty-year reserves.

CMAL and the Alaska lobby were more successful in the Senate. Keeping in mind that economic development in Alaska would be stymied if the Congress remained adamant, Stevens guided a compromise through the legislative process. It would set aside only 104 million acres of new reserves, 15 percent less than Udall's House bill, but more than the 60 million acres that Stevens had hoped for. But it included virtually all of the seven points on the Alaska lobby agenda, points which environmentalists thought would vitiate the concept of preservation in Alaska. Yet the bill included over 56 million acres of new wilderness lands. The Senate passed the bill in August, having first voted to kill Senator Gravel's filibuster.

Stevens warned the House environmentalists that the Senate bill was a "take it or leave it" proposition. Neither he nor Senator Gravel would accept any amendments. In the House, Congressman Udall prepared to stand firm. The Congress and Alaska were at a historic impasse. Stevens had been forced to accept the unthinkable. Americans, through their Congress, were going to demand that Alaska bow to the national will. A significant portion of Alaska was going to be marked "off limits" to exploitation by a pioneer, colonial economy. America was going to have its Alaska environmental crown jewels. This Stevens would accept, but only to a point. This Governor Hammond would accept. Gravel was bludgeoned into acceptance by a cloture vote cutting off his filibuster. Alaska's Congressman Don Young and CMAL would follow Stevens' lead. But would Udall and the Alaska Coalition accept compromise? The environmental leader said no, and there matters stood as the country went to the polls in November 1980.

As in the settlement of Alaska Native land claims, it would be the American people who would resolve this impasse and make the decision on Alaska lands. In the 1980 elections, voters elected Ronald Reagan president and sent a Republican majority to the Senate. When the new Congress took office in January, there would be less sentiment in favor

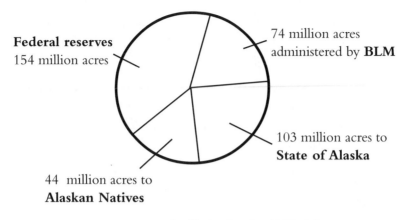

Disposition of public land under ANILCA.

of a strong environmental bill than there had been in the 96th Congress. There was now no chance of getting approval of Udall's H.R. 39. Accepting reality, two weeks after the election Udall asked the House to approve the Senate bill. They did so by voice vote. On December 2, 1980, President Carter signed into law the Alaska National Interest Lands Conservation Act.

"Mr. Udall Gives In," the *Anchorage Times* announced; "he struck his battle flags and gave up the fight." Quoting the Congressman saying that he was "bowing to reality," the paper noted that until Udall's announcement there had been uncertainty, and environmentalists had been calling for "last ditch posturing." Both Udall and Senator Stevens said they would work to correct "deficiencies" in the legislation, of a different sort for each. In Washington, President Carter said of the act, "It is a victory in the long struggle to resolve this issue, and is truly an historic moment in our nation's history."

Udall's disappointment notwithstanding, ANILCA was sweeping legislation, unprecedented in American history and not likely to be repeated. It set aside 104 million acres of Alaska land in a variety of new conservation units; 56.4 million of those acres were classified as wilderness. It provided national park protection to ten new areas and made additions to three existing ones. It added 1.3 million acres to the Tongass Forest, and designated 5.4 million of the forest as wilderness. In the creation of a vast swath of contiguous reserves across the south flank of the Brooks Range and south to the Yukon River, ANILCA brought protection to a significant area of the state previously open to mining and other kinds of entry.

Conservationists in America were initially delighted, even though they did not get a great many areas into the bill they wanted protected. But as they reviewed the bill, some became increasingly dismayed, for what at first appeared to be protection looked on inspection to be riddled with contradictions. Senators Stevens and Gravel and Congressman Young, backed by CMAL and the Alaska lobbyists, had been able to write a great many exceptions into the act, exceptions from the manner in which park and refuge lands were administered in the contiguous states, and exceptions which drew boundaries of one sort or another around lands of economic potential, excluding them from the conservation units. The Alaska Coalition had wanted whole ecosystems preserved, but in many instances these were fractured or incomplete. A number of units that conservationists had wanted designated parks had instead been given a new classification: preserve. This meant that sport hunting and other kinds of activities were permitted in them, an activity banned from parks in other states. Avoiding racial designations, the act allowed traditional backcountry uses, so as not to eliminate subsistence use by rural residents, who were mostly Native. This meant that snow machines, motorboats, and floatplanes, as well as high-powered rifles, chain saws, and even cabins would be tolerated in areas designated wilderness, hardly the "untrammeled" character defined in the 1964 Wilderness Act. In a major concession from the early dreams of many environmentalists, the act allowed prospecting on most land known to have mineral or oil potential. These included such areas as Glacier Bay National Monument where a rich nickel-copper deposit was found in the 1950s, and a bornite (a sulfide of copper) deposit in the Kobuk River drainage. Areas specifically excluded from the act included a world class lead and zinc deposit, Red Dog, on the Arctic Coast north of Kotzebue, a large low-grade molybdenum deposit at Quartz Hill in the Misty Fjords National Monument in the Tongass Forest, a silver and lead deposit at Greens Creek on Admiralty Island, and a gold deposit at Golden Zone. In the Tongass National Forest, where the two pulp mills resulting from the Tongass Timber Act of 1947 operated at Ketchikan and Sitka, the act provided a $40 million annual subsidy for the U.S. Forest Service: Alaska Region. This was to insure timber lease sales, together with forest roads, sufficient to allow 4.5 million board feet of timber to be cut annually, a 35 percent increase in the average annual cut in the previous three decades. No other forest region in the country was so generously supported for timber lease sales. Conservationists considered many of these exceptions as serious flaws in the act.

Other significant aspects of the act also dismayed conservationists. The act guaranteed access by floatplane, motorboat, and snow machine to millions of acres not just for sport hunting, but for other traditional activities as well. Areas could be closed if the access caused adverse impacts, but the right of access is presumed. In addition, access was guaranteed to in-holdings, i.e., already titled, privately held lands, in the national parks and refuges. Consistent with the 1976 NFMA and FLPMA legislation, management plans for the units were to include public hearings. Navigable waters were to be deeded to the state, and access to them guaranteed. In addition, access was to be protected to state lands and waters that lie within federal units or are surrounded by them. Also, mining in the Kantishna Hills district, added to the extension to Denali Park, was to be permitted following appropriate assessment of environmental impacts. In addition, the Secretary of the Interior was to assess the potential for oil development in the coastal plain of the Arctic National Wildlife Refuge, and at his discretion permit exploratory drilling. And Senator Gravel's clause prohibiting further executive withdrawals for conservation exceeding 5,000 acres in Alaska without congressional approval was included in the final bill.

After review of all the exceptions, some critics wondered that it was called a conservation act at all. But most recognized that even though there would be much controversy as the act was implemented, it did provide a framework for preservation in Alaska. President Carter, writing fifteen years after ANILCA, said that it was "one of my proudest accomplishments as President," a sentiment most Americans accepted.

It is not possible to appreciate the impact of ANILCA on Alaska, or to comprehend the vehement opposition to it within the state, without an understanding of the impact of the state's transformation by "Big Oil," the extraordinary amount of money that became available to state government and to the state's citizens, and for business opportunities. Major figures in the federal government spent considerable time in the late 1980s crafting strategies to protect the Alaska environment, while at the same time people in Alaska crafted ways to spend new, unprecedented aggregates of money, much of it on economic development that would impinge on that same environment. Both developments had a direct bearing on the evolution of Native life in Alaska, both the ANCSA corporations and the individual villages. The juxtaposition of these phenomena is fascinating.

To become suddenly super-rich, as Alaska did following authorization and construction of the pipeline and the onset of oil production in 1977, was in some ways to become very confused. The governor and the legislature struggled with mechanisms for controlling and directing the new wealth so that it would not be wasted, but with uneven results. The money helped build material infrastructure that could not have been built otherwise, including roads, schools, libraries, government offices, performing arts centers, and city-owned sports arenas. These were simply extensions of the replication of mainstream American material culture. But they manifested well Alaskans' notions of what sort of society they wished to see develop on the edge of the wilderness. Much of the outrage Alaskans expressed during the battle over the Alaska lands bill stemmed from their anxiety that the opportunity to replicate, to build, would be cut off. With oil money flowing into the state treasury, and with the oil industry expanding in the private sector at a previously unimagined pace, Alaskans saw all around them, daily, the impact of their new wealth. But the examples of oil's impact were at the same time examples of Alaskans' dependence on oil production, and on the forces and people who controlled it. A poignant, revealing moment occurred in Alaska's history in 1969. Soon after ARCO confirmed the magnitude of its North Slope discovery, the state held a new, competitive, North Slope lease sale. Scores of oil companies sought the leases. The competition was aggressive. Company agents studied geology maps, talked with experienced North Slope geologists, spied against competitors, went to absurd lengths to maintain secrecy about their own plans, yet were conspicuous in and around Anchorage, the base of their operations, by their private planes, their Texas and New York attire and swagger, and their furtive mannerisms. September 10, when the bids were opened before a packed crowd in the largest auditorium in the city, was a day of high drama. The proffered leases were for what might be (and turned out to be) some of the richest oil land in the Americas. The bids were high, and the audience gasped audibly as the governor and the state's natural resources commissioner announced one after another outrageously high bid for this and that tract of barren land. At the end of the day, the state had collected $900,220,590 in lease revenue. This was more than three times the total state budget at the time. The state required a 20 percent deposit for each successful bid, so by the session's end, the state treasurer had $180 million in certified and cashier's checks in his briefcase. This was years ahead of computer transfers of assets, so the state had chartered a United Airlines DC-8, which was kept running and ready from mid-afternoon at the

Anchorage International Airport, to rush the money to San Francisco where it could begin to earn $45,000 a day in interest.

Alaskans were spectators at this bizarre series of events. They could do little but watch, and collect the money. With that money lay their hopes, but they had no influence over who might bid how much on which tract with what implications. Photos of the officials seated on the stage of the auditorium, with a large chart behind them showing the cumulative income total, are common in representations of Alaska's modern development. They note the beginning of the modern oil era. But they state a none-too-subtle subtext as well: Alaska's dependence. With the dependence came insecurity, for the oil industry is, for all practical purpose, Alaska's only private economy. This perception colors every Alaskan's sense of well-being, and for the 70 percent of the population living in the urban corridor, it is a sword of Damocles hanging over the future.

In the late 1970s, examples of Alaskans' dependence on oil were no longer new. Every new expenditure of state revenue, every new construction project undertaken by the state, or by the oil industry, or in commercial and real estate development, reminded Alaskans of their dependence, for about every one it could be observed, whether true or not, that it wouldn't be happening except for oil. And the reminders were everywhere, for the amount of oil revenue dwarfed prediction. Thus, Alaskans inexorably became wedded to the oil industry. It is essential to grasp the depth and comprehensive nature of the dependence on oil in Alaska, and the citizens' recognition of their dependence, to appreciate its impact on the society.

It is no wonder, then, that relief was palpable in Alaska after the passage of ANILCA. The act provided the state with its final selections under the statehood act, confirmed the Native selections provided by ANCSA, and eliminated any land title questions that might impede economic development. Oil had been flowing since 1977, and state spending reached an all-time high. Though many in the state berated national environmental leaders for the delay in construction of the pipeline and the onset of oil production, the state benefited tremendously. The Arab-Israeli War and the OPEC embargo that generated support for the pipeline authorization act pushed world oil prices very high. Since part of Alaska's tax revenue was linked to the price of the oil, state revenue soared accordingly. Then, a war between Iran and Iraq exacerbated a shortage in world oil production, driving the price still higher. By 1980 the world price of oil was approaching $40 a barrel, ten times the price in 1970. During the

Iran–Iraq War, Alaska revenue topped $4.5 billion for 1971. No one knew exactly how much money was coming into the state treasury, and no one know what to do with however much it was. The circumstances made possible all manner of government projects, some successful, others ill-judged. The period between 1975 and 1985 was truly the "golden decade" in Alaska, far more significant in facilitating the transport to the state of America's materialist-oriented consumer culture than any other in Alaska history.

Democrats controlled the state legislature at the height of the boom in 1981, and party leaders froze both Republicans and junior members of their own party out of the decisions on state spending. Hammond's Republican administration had difficulty getting accurate information on the revenue stream, generating distrust. A young maverick Democrat in the state House quietly formed an insurgent coalition that took control of the legislature away from the Democratic leaders. The coup was apparently a first in American state legislative politics; no other state legislature had changed its leadership without changing its membership. The insurgent leader, Russ Meekins, Jr., then forged a way to deal with the surplus oil tax revenues. The governor, the state House, and the state Senate each would each take a third of the excess funds and spend them however they wished, with no questions asked by the other two. All parties agreed, and the big spend-off was on. Overnight the capital budget mushroomed to double the operating budget. Individual legislators took home nearly a million dollars each to their districts. Many projects, no matter how well designed, succumbed to misdirections and over-budgeting.

The governor, for example, designed two related developmental initiatives to generate agricultural industry in Alaska. One was an attempt to develop a barley industry, another a massive dairy farm project. Both failed miserably, and very visibly. But there were successes as well, and two are especially noteworthy. In 1983 Governor William Sheffield initiated purchase of the Alaska Railroad from the federal government. In the modern era there was no reason for the federal government to support the line, and rising state oil revenue provided an opportunity for the state to take it over. The independent American Railroad Association set the fair market value of the 483-mile road at $22.3 million. The transfer of ownership took place in 1985, the legislature forming a state-owned corporation to run it, the Alaska Railroad Corporation. The railroad has operated at a profit since the state acquired it; the 1999 profit was $9.9 million on revenues of $88.9 million and total assets of $223 million.

In another imaginative use of the unprecedented revenues, the state undertook to construct a high school in every community with fifteen students. In the early 1970s, a number of Natives brought suit to force the construction of such schools. Most Alaska Native youngsters had to travel to the BIA (later state) school at Mt. Edgecumbe at Sitka, or to a BIA school out of state, or board with families in Anchorage or Fairbanks for secondary education. Alaska Legal Services filed a suit on behalf of Native children. The state supreme court denied that the state constitution obligates the state to provide a school in every community. But the attorney general thought it not an inappropriate use of state funds. Initially projected to cost $30 million, by its completion in the 1980s the program had cost $150 million. Neither of these programs could have contemplated had not oil prices skyrocketed in the late 1970s and early 1980s.

But each of these projects and many, many more reminded Alaskans daily of their dependence on oil. Nor was there anything to mitigate that dependence, for the schemes the state initiated to free Alaska from reliance on outside capital mostly failed, highlighting the inability to achieve the promise of statehood. This was not a reality many Alaskans could accept. Many found solace in conspiracy theory, and their favorite targets were the federal government and environmentalists.

Several events in the early 1980s demonstrated that the habit of oppositional thinking, particularly that directed at the federal government, was as strong as ever. One was the "tundra rebellion." In 1979 the Nevada legislature initiated the so-called "sagebrush rebellion" by enacting a law asserting a state claim to all the federally owned land in the state—83 percent in Nevada, more by percentage than any other state. The measure further called upon the state, when in possession of the land, to provide for its transfer to individual ownership. The Nevada law had no legal or constitutional standing, but it articulated the anger and frustration of many western land users with the changing land management policies that were a part of the environmental revolution. It also reflected the work of James Watt of the Mountain States Legal Defense Fund, who argued that the origin and content of federal public land laws were assailable.

Still chafing from a decade of confrontation with the federal government over Native claims, the pipeline, and conservation withdrawals, in 1980 the Alaska legislature passed a resolution establishing a "statehood commission" to examine the relationship between the state and the federal government, and "to recommend appropriate changes in the relationship of the people of Alaska to the United States."

To some degree the creation of the commission reflected the vulnerability and naiveté of Alaskans, particularly their susceptibility to manipulation by politicians who either do or do not know the history of federal support for Alaska and the constitutional history of federal sovereignty. There was little the commission could do, of course, except fund studies by scholars, which it did. The commission's final recommendations counseled continued union with the United States.

Nonetheless, in 1982, the state legislature passed a "sagebrush rebellion" bill, declaring that 56 million acres of BLM land in Alaska was state-owned land. As had the Nevada law, the Alaska statute declared that traditional use by state residents had persisted over a sufficient period of time that the state had de facto title to the land. Like the Nevada statute, the Alaska law was, of course, not constitutional. But that did not prevent lawmakers and other state opinion leaders from maintaining the anti-federal rhetoric that had dominated public discourse throughout the region's history, renewed with vigor during the decade of the 1970s.

⋊⋉

The most important project generated by the revenue stream of the "golden decade" was the Alaska Permanent Fund. It would fulfill a historic Alaskan dream, to capture directly for Alaskans some of the money generated by resource exploitation. At the same time it would change the character of Alaska politics. And it can be argued that it exacerbated both Alaskans' oppositional mode of thinking and their appetite for consumer goods and culture.

At Governor Hammond's urging, voters in 1976 amended the state constitution to establish a state permanent investment fund into which would be deposited 25 percent of petroleum lease bonuses, royalties, and rentals. At the same time, and as an incentive to persuade voters to accept the fund idea, the legislature repealed the state income tax. The state has never had a sales tax. While the permanent fund was constitutionally created, its management was left to the legislature, which created the Alaska Permanent Fund Corporation to manage the fund conservatively as a savings account, making income-producing investments. Through careful management, and "inflation proofing," i.e., redepositing a portion of the earnings equal to the rate of inflation, the Fund grew by the year 2001 to $27 billion.

By 1980 the fund had generated sufficient earnings that the legislature enacted a program to distribute a portion of the earnings each year to Alaska residents. The dividend would be the most efficient way of giving Alaskans a benefit of the use and depletion of their oil. It would also generate a constituent interest in the fund, particularly in preventing the legislature from appropriating the annual earnings.

Following a successful suit over discrimination in the distribution of the dividend earnings based on length of residence, the legislature moved quickly to put a distribution program in place. The law, enacted in 1982, requires half of Fund earnings to be distributed as a dividend on a per capita basis to all resident citizens. Dividends have been paid every year since 1982, ranging upward from $800. In 2000, the dividend was nearly $2,000. For urban, middle class families, the dividend is a welcome bonus. For Alaska Native villagers with low cash incomes who depend on subsistence for a substantial portion of their annual food supply, and who may include a large number of family members, the dividend may represent much of the family income in any given year. The program is extraordinarily popular with Alaskans, making any attempt by legislators and politicians to use any portion of Fund earnings for government spending political suicide. In 1988 Governor Steve Cowper tried to generate support for an education endowment funded by a portion of Permanent Fund earnings. He was unsuccessful. In September 2000, the state legislature placed an advisory question on the general election ballot, asking voters if Fund earnings should be used for state expenses, since the state budget had run a deficit for several years. An overpowering majority, 80 percent, said "No!"

Since its creation in 1976, and increasingly as the annual dividend has grown, the Alaska Permanent Fund is a constant reminder to Alaskans of their dependence on oil extraction for the state's economy. But there are other persistent reminders, as well. One is the price of oil. A portion of the taxes collected from oil production in Alaska is linked to the wholesale price of Alaskan crude on the world market; a higher oil price generates more tax revenue. Alaskans are in a paradoxical situation. Suffering in the form of higher gasoline prices in the contiguous states yields joy in Alaska over more tax revenue and a higher annual Permanent Fund dividend check.

Any fall in the price of oil causes anguish in Alaska, for not only may a sustained or a calamitously low price reduce the size of the dividend but, as Alaskans learned in 1985, it may severely, negatively affect the entire Alaska economy. From a high of $40 per barrel in 1981, and a steady rate of about $27 a barrel in 1985, by 1986 oil prices had fallen to less than $15. The impact on the state's economy was devastating. The value of state general fund revenues fell from $4.1 billion in 1984 to $2.9 billion in 1986 and $2.1 billion in 1988. State general appropriations fell from $4.3 billion in 1985 to $3.1 billion in 1986, and $2.4 billion in 1988. Capital expenditures from the appropriations fell from $1.7 billion in 1985 by a third, to $606 million in 1986, and $214 million in 1988. By 1990 they had dipped to $143 million. As these numbers indicate, state government officials acted quickly to cut capital spending, but that was hardly enough to stave off the effects of the crisis. The deep budget cuts necessary in the operating budget meant a widespread loss of jobs, reduced incomes, and loss of business and property value. Of fifteen banking institutions in the state, nine went under. Federal banking inspectors moved from one bankruptcy to another as if moving through the wreckage of a natural disaster.

Without jobs and in a failing economy, many Alaskans had to face the unthinkable. Between 1985 and 1990, sixty thousand more people left the state than entered it, nearly 15 percent of the total population. Many simply left their homes and much of their belongings, put the key in the lock, and drove away. Both personal and business bankruptcies hit record highs in 1987. Many residential properties had been financed by a state-owned housing authority, which had been pressured by the legislature into a mobile home financing program. Since the mobile home market serviced people who could not generate financing for more expensive, more substantial homes, that market suffered the most in the crash. The state lost $1.1 billion in mortgage foreclosures. In terms of human lives, the cost was incalculable: dreams shattered, emotional stress, dislocation, debt, disruption. Banks did what they to help. Many sent good borrowers away with letters explaining the collapse and urging other lenders to recognize them as good credit risks. Sympathetic hold-outs placed signs along the highway out of Anchorage: "Good bye: We'll Miss You."

The drop in oil prices in 1985-86 was the result of a glut of world supply, resulting from the end of the Iran-Iraq war and a substantial increase in production and export by the oil-producing nations. American oil companies had little to do with generating the crisis, and could do little to mitigate it. Neither could the American government. Alaska state government weathered the crisis by cutting capital spending and by beginning to run deficit budgets. The world price of oil stabilized by the end of the 1980s, and windfall profits, settlement of tax disputes with the oil companies, and streamlined state government helped the

Urban Anchorage; largest building at left is Phillips Petroleum's regional headquarters. (Courtesy Anchorage Daily News, photograph by Erik Hill)

state muddle through. But by 2001 the state had yet to balance its budget, or to devise a long-range spending plan.

Like the North Slope lease sale of 1969, the crash of 1986–87 lives vividly in Alaska memories. The memory of the crash reminds Alaskans of the fragility of the regional economy, so heavily dependent on a single source of tax revenue, of jobs, of continuity. And it generates and exacerbates a sense of insecurity. The images of people walking away from their homes, of people driving out of Alaska because they had no jobs and no livelihood, of life savings drained as people scrambled to save their futures, becomes quickly linked to concern over world oil prices and supplies and the commitment of the oil companies in Alaska to continued production and exploration. For the few who have knowledge of Alaska's colonial past, it confirms the state's colonial present. And it focuses attention toward the Permanent Fund dividend, which has increasingly been seen as a just reward for living in Alaska.

The Alaska Native Claims Settlement Act in 1971 included a twenty-year period for launching the new regional and village development corporations. Certain restrictions applied during the transition period that would expire afterward, including a prohibition on sale of stock to non-Natives. As the expiration neared, Native leaders became increasingly alarmed at the prospect of non-Natives gaining control over the corporations. Retaining control over Native lands while insuring a permanent income and providing an option of traditional or modern lifestyles, or both, was one of the fundamental objectives of the act. Non-native control of the corporations would jeopardize that. In 1989, the AFN endorsed and lobbied through Congress a collection of amendments that maintained the restriction on stock sale, subject to a vote of a majority of stockholders, and also authorized the corporations to issue new stock to persons born after 1971.

By the 1990s, many Natives had begun to construct various syntheses that melded Native and non-Native cultures. Some utilized the economic benefits of the act to pursue education and urban employment and opportunity while maintaining connections with ancestral villages, returning for visits or extended stays, and gathering with friends and relatives to renew traditional rituals in their urban homes. Others lived and worked in villages, but utilized stock and Permanent Fund dividends and other income to spend time in Alaska's cities, or in places outside Alaska.

But the adoption of capitalism changes the nature of choices. And some of the choices left, when exercised, may have troubling consequences. Writer Larry Pynn and others have described an unfortunate circumstance at the village of Hoonah, on Icy Strait in Southeast Alaska not far from Glacier Bay. Hoonah received 23,000 acres of land in ANCSA, which the village corporation sold to the regional corporation, Sealaska, Inc., investing the proceeds in a number of successful ventures. Today village stockholders receive good dividends from the investments. In the meantime, Sealaska, which received 400,000 acres for itself under ANCSA, some of it adjacent to the land it bought from the village corporation, began to log the forest across the bay from Hoonah village. Sealaska is chartered under the laws of the State of Alaska, and as its land is private, it is not subject to the environmental or trade regulations that govern timber sales on nearby Tongass National Forest lands. The result is that Hoonah villagers now look out across their bay, Port Frederick, at a giant scar, miles of clear-cut hillside. Some call it greed. Others say that forests in this region grow back more quickly than nearly anywhere else. Most villagers in Hoonah have come to terms with the choice they have made. But one of the consequences of that choice is evident daily, across Port Frederick.

A romantic view of Native culture assumes Natives are natural environmentalists. Others have argued that the ecological Indian is a non-Native myth. Early criticism of ANCSA focused on the alien nature of capitalism in Native culture, and one analyst called the act the most efficient vehicle imaginable for cultural genocide. In Alaska, the melding of traditional and western culture has rejected one or the other, but proceeded on the principle of amalgam, the survival of both. Thus it is not surprising that the mistakes as well as the triumphs of each cultural mode should be manifest.

Doyon, Ltd., is the Interior Alaska Native economic regional development corporation; its shareholders are Athabaskan Indians. The corporation's profit on investments in 2000 was about $20 million. It is the largest private landholder in Alaska, with 12.5 million acres. The corporation has carried out a number of mineral surveys on its land. One of Doyon's investments is Doyon Drilling, an oil field drilling company with major contracts on Alaska's North Slope. Doyon Drilling contributes about half of Doyon's corporate profits. The company has a reputation for competence and reliability. But in 1998, Doyon Drilling was fined $3 million for illegally dumping contaminated and toxic drill wastes down drill shafts at British Petroleum's Endicott Island oil site over a four-year period. Doyon Drilling advertises that it is "an exemplary company," one "that brings Alaska Native men and women into a career opportunity on the North Slope." When the sentence was handed down by the court, Doyon president Morris Thompson said, "We're saddened that these mistakes have taken place...We can be a company that doesn't get into this kind of predicament. We have learned a lot in this process." Thompson and the board of directors were most likely good land stewards. But they also established a company structure in which profit overrode sensitivity to the integrity of the land Doyon managers made the same decision Alaska territorial leaders made in 1947 when they supported opening the Tongass National Forest to timber lease sales and the construction of pulp mills in 1947; they put economic development ahead of other considerations. If the lesson was that Natives should learn the corporate culture, they learned the lesson well.

Alaska Native cultures did not have broad experience with corporate capitalism, though it would be a mistake to conclude that corporate organization and capitalist enterprise were unknown and alien in 1971 when ANCSA was passed. The acculturation of Alaska Natives began under the Russians, before the American purchase, and as we have seen above, by the 1920s Tlingit and Haida people were well versed in the modes and mores of western economics and politics. Other Native groups were not far behind. Communities as widely separated as Karluk on Kodiak Island, Venetie and Arctic Village in the southeast Brooks Range, and Tetlin in the upper Tanana River drainage successfully organized for political action on the question of reservations in the 1940s. Eskimos were particularly effective in protesting Project Chariot in the 1950s. And Howard Rock, editor of the *Tundra Times*, superbly orchestrated a consciousness-raising agenda that helped alert Eskimo, Athabaskan, and Aleut communities of the threat to their lands, traditions, and cultures presented by the state's land selections after 1959.

But the magnitude and intricacy of corporate investment strategies required of the Native leadership cadre as the ANCSA corporations were created after 1971 surpassed the capability of many Native communities, and for that matter, the advisors they brought from within Alaska and across the nation. Several of the regional corporations made major missteps, as did a number of the village entities. Assessing the impact of the settlement act in one hundred Alaska villages in 1985, Canadian jurist Thomas Berger found that failures by corporation officers had led to disaffection among many villagers, who thought they had got nothing in compensation for the loss of Native land represented by the extinguishment of title in the claims act.

Senator Ted Stevens stepped in to remedy the situation. In 1986 he wrote into the tax law a provision allowing Alaska Native corporations to sell their net operating losses to another company. The buyers could then write off those losses against their profits. The measure attracted interest across the country, setting of a frenzy of negotiations with Native corporation leaders. The list of companies interested in the deal included some of America's best-known brand names, including General Motors, Sara Lee, Pillsbury, Procter and Gamble, Marriott, and advertisers Young & Rubicam. Initial estimates suggested the total of such sales would be $300 or $400 million, but by 1988 they had already topped $1 billion. Since the deal was available to any Alaska Native corporation, even healthy ones took advantage of the opportunity to better their circumstances. In the meantime, financially troubled Doyon, Inc., sold Campbell Soup Co. $39 million in losses, saving the food producer about $44 million on its 1987 tax bill. Native corporations typically got about 30 cents on the dollar for their losses. By 1988 the $1 billion in sales had cost the U.S.

treasury about $400 million, and the Senate decided to call a halt to the practice; the program was terminated on December 31. Without question, the deal gave new life to Alaska Native corporations. Several had been facing possible bankruptcy. The big winners were Sealaska Corporation, which gained about $350 million, and a number of southeast village corporations, all of which had developed losses when prices in the timber industry fell to historic post-war low levels.

The episode demonstrated again that Native Alaskans had fully learned the mechanisms of corporate management. They were as much at ease in the boardroom, the courtroom, and the Senate office as on the river or in an umiak, or hunting a bear or moose. When Congress passed the claims settlement act in 1971, many analysts argued that the corporate model of economic and political organization was alien to traditional Native cultures, and would hasten the acculturation and destruction of those cultures. As noted previously, at least one writer called ANCSA the greatest act of cultural genocide in the nation's history. But such a judgment seems to deny Native people the right to choose their destiny. Many Native leaders have defended ANCSA on the realistic grounds that material advancement for Alaska Native people demands economic empowerment. ANCSA was designed to provide that empowerment. Not only have Alaska Natives become equal economic players in Alaska, and outside Alaska, through the mechanisms of ANCSA, but, perhaps miraculously, they also have managed to retain the option to maintain a wilderness life style to some degree. But sustaining that option in the future represents a formidable challenge.

The implications of the Alaska lands act for the sustainability of Alaska Native village life would be a major focus of the 1990s, as federal land and resource managers set about to implement ANICA in the context of the transformation of Alaska by "Big Oil."

6

Debacle: The *Exxon Valdez,* the Tongass Forest, and the ELF

⊱⊰

In his study of technology, conservation, and the frontier in Alaska, historian Peter A. Coates discussed Daniel Boorstin's definitions of the terms "booster" and "boomer," the latter term used to describe some western settlers, not to be confused with the later "baby boomer." Boosters, Boorstin argued, took a longer view than boomers, who, like Richard White's "modern migrants," sought to increase their material worth through exploitation of natural resources in the West, and return with their new wealth to the more settled regions. In Alaska, Coates suggests, the distinction had no real meaning, for both wanted unrestricted access to the region's natural resources. The purpose for both was to fund and facilitate the replication in Alaska of modern American material, consumer culture. As Coates notes, Richard C. Wade and Earl Pomeroy both called attention to the role of the city in developing the West, usually growing in population more rapidly than new settlement in the hinterland. The towns and cities were where the most rapid and complete replication of American material culture took place. Most people moving west did not settle in the hinterland; they settled in the cities. Alaska followed that pattern. Anchorage was a town of twenty-two hundred in 1940; by 1950 the population was thirty-two thousand, a fourteen-fold increase. By 1960, ninety thousand people, 40 percent of the new state's population lived there, and by 1970, nearly half. As in many western states, Idaho,

Oregon, Washington, half the population of the state is now crowded into one urban concentration, and, as noted above, in Alaska 70 percent live in an urban corridor along the coast and along the rail belt from Seward to Interior Fairbanks.

The boosters who promoted such growth perceived themselves to be in a continuing struggle of vast proportions, as Ernest Gruening portrayed it in his polemical history of the territory. Their primary opponent was not the wilderness, however. The boosters did not doubt their capacity to subdue wilderness, quickly and efficiently. In their lifetimes they had seen the airplane, the snow machine, satellite communication, and a host of other technologies adapted swiftly to the harshest northern conditions. Technology was their agent in subduing the wilderness. And once statehood had been achieved, representing the defeat of its most visible opponent, the canned salmon industry, the boosters did not perceive absentee capital as an impediment. To the contrary, they perhaps naively saw corporate investors as partners.

Instead, their chief opponent, they were convinced, was government, for it was government that controlled access to the land and its resources. The battles over Project Chariot, Rampart Dam, the Arctic National Wildlife Range, the pipeline, and the Alaska lands act had all been about access to wilderness resources by a local/absentee partnership committed to settling the frontier. Allied with the government were environmentalists, who, the boosters were persuaded, wanted selfishly to deny the pioneer population their just due as Americans and as adventurers on the northern frontier, and to lock up the wilderness for its own, decidedly un-American ideas. Wilderness, the boosters insisted in the tradition of Progressive conservation, was waste. As Walter Hickel said, "we can't just let nature run wild."

It was axiomatic among the boosters that Alaska's resources were infinite. Several significant environmental episodes in the late 1980s showed that this belief was unchanged in the modern era in Alaska. A prime example was a new battle over the Tongass National Forest. Although the Alaska lands act set aside 5.4 million acres of the Tongass Forest as wilderness, it did not alter the terms of the 1947 Tongass Timber Act, which mandated that 4.5 billion board feet of timber be made available each decade regardless of market conditions. It also left the fifty-year contracts for the two pulp mills intact. As a trade-off for establishment of the wilderness, Congress guaranteed an annual $40 million subsidy for construction of logging roads and other timber sale preparations.

Environmentalists had been unhappy with these provisions since the passage of the lands act. The Tongass Forest contained the last extensive stands of old-growth timber in the national forest system. Much of it was available for harvesting under ANILCA. During the 1980s, trees in the forest sold for as little as $3 per 1,000 board feet while the same timber sold on the open market fetched $200. Much of the timber produced in the mills was exported to the Far East; the Sitka mill was Japanese owned. A new coalition of national environmental groups, again headed by the Sierra Club, decided to make the Tongass Forest a national issue. Publication and education were again the primary weapons. The Sierra Club book on the Tongass was a stunning photographic achievement, presenting the forest in all of its grandeur and poignancy. The Forest Service itself published several lavishly illustrated bulletins describing the wilderness area of the forest and suggesting the compatibility of scientific forest management and wilderness protection. The Southeast Alaska Conservation Council published a report that called attention to the record of pollution by the pulp mills, Louisiana Pacific at Ketchikan and Alaska Lumber and Pulp at Sitka. The record was dismal. In addition, SEACC demonstrated that salmon buffers were inadequate or missing, road building seemed on a par with Orange County, California, and the deer population was faltering.

The Alaska Loggers Association presented the position of many Alaskans. In a folksy portrayal of the "working forest," K. A. Soderberg and Jackie DuRette, wives of active Tongass loggers, defended the development of the forest by focusing on the work histories of individual harvesters and gypo logging operations. *People of the Tongass* argued that the loggers had a high level of environmental sensitivity. Soderberg, the primary author, argued that logging had no environmental impact on the forest, that in fact, the harvest improved the forest's health. The pulp mills and a major sawmill in Wrangell provided hundreds of jobs, Soderberg noted, suggesting that without the industry, she and others like her would have to abandon Alaska. The mills had proven, she insisted, that they operated well within the limits of allowable pollution and other restrictions.

By 1989 the battle had become intense, and environmentalists in Congress introduced new legislation to change the ANILCA provisions for the Tongass Forest. The Sierra Club and others in the coalition had succeeded in making "old-growth timber" a national environmental battle cry. Both the House Interior and Agriculture committees developed bills to rewrite the Tongass provisions in ANILCA. In hearings, Alaskans stressed the necessity of the forest cut for the economic stability of Southeast, while environmentalists decried the eradication of an irreplaceable national treasure. Alaska's Senator Frank Murkowski charged the environmental lobby with conspiracy to use the issue to build up their memberships, and with pulling the wool over Americans' eyes in regard to the compatibility of timber harvest and environmental values. National editorial opinion favored reform of the act, however. Timothy Egan, *New York Times* writer in Seattle, captured the essence of national outrage in a column in which he pointed out that the U.S. Forest Service was selling five-hundred-year trees on the Tongass Forest for the price of a MacDonald's "Big Mac."

For Alaskans, several developments exacerbated the stress associated with the struggle. First, the bottom fell out of the timber market. In most years of the 1980s, the market was so depressed that only 250 million board feet of the 450 million mandated were harvested. The Forest Service prepared timber sales only to have no bidders. At the same time, the Native corporations were beginning to harvest their lands. Their production exceeded Forest Service predictions by 40 percent. Also, the salmon harvest increased dramatically, increasing the utilization of waters in the forest, and tourism grew at unprecedented rates, bringing unexpected and sometimes unwanted peering eyes and cameras to the clear-cut areas

Polls in Alaska showed that a majority favored cutting the forest. Alaska Senators Stevens and Murkowski fought against revising the law, and press reports in Alaska suggested support for this position. They were able to delay the bill, but the pressure was simply too great for them to be able to defeat it.

The final bill, the Tongass Timber Reform Act of 1990, retained the fifty-year contracts, which House members had wanted to eliminate. But it ended the $40 million annual special appropriation for lease sale preparation, and removed the 4.5 billion board feet harvest target each decade. Also, the Forest Service was directed to sell logs at a profitable price. The act protected an additional one million acres of the 16.7-million-acre forest from timber cutting, designating 300,000 acres of that as wilderness and thereby protecting the last stands of virgin old growth in the United States.

The reform act brought much greater environmental protection to the Tongass Forest. But its economic consequences were not long in becoming manifest. On July 1, 1993, the Sitka mill, Alaska Pulp Company, owned and operated by Alaska Lumber and Pulp, ceased operation and closed. Four hundred people lost their jobs. Sitka's economy had become substantially diversified, primarily as a consequence of a booming tourist industry tied partly to increased cruise ship traffic, and analysts calculated that the mill had supported 20 percent of the town's economy. Mill owners initially blamed the closure on Forest Service alterations in the fifty-year contracts. But what the Forest Service had demanded was compliance with tighter environmental restrictions in harvesting, and particularly, in the operation of the mill. The mill was a chronic polluter. Disputes between Alaska Pulp and federal regulators over the amount of pollutants dumped by the mill reached back to the 1970s and included several prior "settlements." The company had previously paid penalties totaling $721,500 and signed an order promising to stop polluting. In part the Forest Service was responding to pressure from the Environmental Protection Agency (EPA). In 1986 the EPA had threatened to close the mill if the pollution did not stop. But records revealed that the mill had resumed illegal discharges within a month of signing the order. Soon after the reform act passed, the EPA cited the mill again, and levied a $1.27 million fine. The EPA demanded several design changes at the mill, and the installation of expensive scrubbing equipment. Mill owners decided not to comply. Instead, they closed the mill.

The scenario was repeated at Ketchikan, where, on September 30, 1997, Louisiana Pacific Corporation (LPC) decided to close its mill rather than spend an estimated $200 million on pollution controls. The Ketchikan mill had never met environmental standards, piling up hundreds of violations. LPC had paid more than $6 million in fines and collected fourteen criminal pollution convictions, one of them a felony charge. Toxic sludge in the cove at the mill had reached a depth of 20 feet.

LPC played hardball. In hearings in Sen. Frank Murkowski's Energy and Natural Resources Committee, the company demanded a reversion to pre-reform bill conditions for marketing timber (i.e., below market prices) before they would guarantee to continue operating. The demand was unreasonable; Murkowski could not go back and ask Congress to undo the reform act. It appeared to be an attempt to blame the Forest Service and the new legislation for the mill's demise. In any case, LPC came away without assurances, and shut down its operation.

Ketchikan's economy, like that of Sitka, had become more diverse, also primarily because of a substantial increase in summer cruise traffic. Huge cruise expedition ships disgorge thousands of tourists into the downtown business district of Ketchikan every summer day, a phenomenon that raises new questions about Alaska culture. But tourism in the Ketchikan economy helped to ease the impact of the mill's closure. In addition, Murkowski was able to direct $110 million in federal funds over four years to offset timber job losses in both Sitka and Ketchikan, and in both cities the state provided funds for job training and counseling. Contrary to the dire predictions of some, both communities were able to weather the economic disruption.

For Alaskans committed to development, the Tongass Timber Reform Act represented a defeat. Passage of the act likely did hasten closure of the mills, for the corporate owners understood the magnitude of support for the bill, doubtless correctly, as a measure of the approval of both the concept of wilderness and of firm enforcement of environmental laws. Once again, Alaskans had misjudged the strength of the national commitment to environmental values.

For environmentalists, the battle over the Tongass could not have come at a more auspicious time. Not only was there no significant demand for the timber at the time of the new Tongass debate, but an environmental explosion had occurred in Alaska of such magnitude that anything dealing with the frontier state had come under the closest, most aggressive scrutiny. The *Exxon Valdez* had run aground.

The *Exxon Valdez* oil spill in Prince William Sound on March 24, 1989, is one of the most significant environmental events in modern times. Because of its magnitude and location, the spill transcended normal reactions to environmental issues. It was the largest oil spill in United States history: 10.8 million gallons. Though it only ranks thirty-fourth among world oil spills, it is generally considered to be the most damaging to the environment. Prince William Sound was a pristine, unique, rich natural ecosystem of about two million acres. A spill of this magnitude in such a place would have been counted a disaster under any circumstances. Coming, as it did, after American environmental consciousness had matured in the 1960s and 1970s, embracing a more protective view of wilderness, it stood as confirmation of the legitimacy of environmental protection and of environmentalists' more dire forecasts. This was particularly true once the causes of the spill had been analyzed. They included the failure of a third mate to properly maneuver the tanker, probably due to fatigue and excessive work load; failure of the master to provide a proper navigation watch, possibly due to impairment from alcohol; failure of the Exxon Shipping Co. to supervise the master and provide a rested and sufficient crew; failure of the U.S. Coast Guard to provide an effective traffic system; and lack of effective pilot and escort services. Three of the five causes were the responsibility of Exxon Corporation, and could appropriately be ascribed to corporate greed. The other two were the responsibility of the U.S. Coast Guard and the State of Alaska Department of Environmental Conservation. Testimony at the state's trial of the tanker captain suggested that both the Coast Guard and the State of Alaska had accepted corporation assurances that tankers were being operated safely through state waters, and that proper precautions had been made to cope with emergencies. Neither of those assurances was true.

The 987-foot *Exxon Valdez* departed the Trans-Alaska Pipeline terminal at Valdez at 9:12 P.M. March 23, 1989. Fully loaded, the 55-million-gallon (1.26 million barrels) tanker drafted 55 feet. After clearing Valdez Narrows, where the shipping channel narrows to one-half mile, the local pilot left the vessel. With Captain Joseph Hazelwood in command of the wheelhouse, and Helmsman Harry Claar steering, the tanker sailed on into the ten-mile-wide Coast Guard-designated shipping lane, but soon encountered icebergs. Hazelwood ordered Claar to take the tanker out of the designated channel to go around them. He then left the bridge to go to his cabin, leaving precise instructions on the exact point at which to turn the vessel back into the designated lanes. The time was about 11:30 P.M. Third Mate Gregory Cousins took control of the wheelhouse and Helmsman Robert Kagan took over the wheel. Kagan and Cousins failed to turn the vessel at the appointed spot, and the ship continued on its diversion course under automatic pilot. At about midnight, a single watch on the forward part of the vessel noted that a channel light that was supposed to be to starboard of the vessel was actually to port. She alerted the helm. Kagan and Cousins immediately attempted to turn the wheel to correct the course, but could not because the automatic pilot was still engaged. Just as they freed the wheel from the autopilot and began to make the turn to port, the ship "fetched up," in Hazelwood's memorable phrase, on Bligh Reef in Prince William Sound. The time was 12:04 A.M. Good Friday. The tanker traveled about six hundred feet after striking the underwater reef, tearing a gash that opened about half the holding tanks along one side. Oil poured into Prince William Sound.

Everything that could go wrong did so. Hazelwood notified the Coast Guard at Valdez, which notified the Alyeska Pipeline Company, who had responsibility under the state's oil spill response plan, to deploy containment booms to keep the oil from spreading and skimmers to begin to collect the oil from the surface of the sea. But these were not in the storage area where they were supposed to be, or were so loaded over with miscellaneous equipment that they could not be retrieved. For two days the ship leaked oil while Exxon Corporation, the Coast Guard, and the State of Alaska frantically attempted to get containment equipment to the site. Then a spring storm hit the Sound. Containment was impossible during the storm, which pushed the oil along the shoreline of the Sound, onto the many islands within, and out along the mainland coast. Moving in a southwesterly direction, the oil spread along 1,300 miles of undulating shoreline, oiling 200 shoreline miles of beaches heavily, and oiling lightly all the way to Chignik, an Alutiq village on the Alaska Peninsula 460 miles from the spill site.

The impact was devastating. Probably two hundred fifty thousand seabirds of various species were killed, twenty-eight hundred sea otters, three hundred harbor seals, two hundred fifty bald eagles, as many as twenty-two killer whales, and billions of salmon and herring eggs. Most of the dead animals sunk. Searchers found the carcasses of more than thirty-five thousand birds and a thousand sea otters. It is noteworthy that the current sea otter population of the Sound is still substantial. Two species, the river otter and bald eagle, have been declared recovered from the effects of the spill. Nine are documented as recovering, including sea otter, clams, and marbled murrelets. Eight species are not recovering, including harbor seals, common loons, harlequin ducks, and three species of cormorants, and the status of four is unknown.

Several Native villages suffered losses as a result of the spill. The village of Chenega Bay lay directly in the path of the spreading oil. Once equipment had been located and assembled, workers from the state quickly placed surface booms across the entrance to the bay in which the village was located, and little oil contaminated the bay or the village beaches. But shellfish, fish, and birds that the villagers relied upon for food were substantially damaged. More important, the largest generator of cash income in the village was commercial fishing. For several seasons, the salmon that villagers would normally have harvested were declared unfit to take. Other villages, Tatitlek, Eyak, Port Graham, English Bay, and Seldovia, had to deal with the same impact. But the spill was especially cruel for Chenega Bay, for the village there was a new one, relocated after the devastating 1964 earthquake had destroyed the original village. At that time, villagers had fled to the hills above the shoreline in time to watch the tsunami generated by the quake sweep into the bay and inundate their houses. Now, twenty-five years later, they watched as the beaches outside Chenega Bay were swept with the black oil. Despite the clean up, and assurances from state and federal biologists, villagers at Chenega are not convinced that there are no long-lasting effects on the subsistence resources they gather from the Sound.

Alaskans deplored the devastation, along with the nation. Democratic Governor Steve Cowper, a reserved Fairbanks attorney and former chair of the House Finance Committee, steered the state deftly through the crisis. He was highly critical of the Exxon Corporation, and disdainful of its attempts to pass the blame for the tragedy to the Coast Guard and the state, and to diffuse responsibility through the various companies in the Alyeska consortium that ran the pipeline and the Valdez shipping terminal. The state successfully prosecuted Captain Hazelwood for illegally discharging oil, the only statute that applied, aside from operating an ocean vessel while intoxicated, a charge on which a jury acquitted him. He was fined $50,000, and ordered to complete one thousand hours of community service in Alaska. The state worked with the federal government on a settlement of criminal charges and civil damages, which totaled over $1 billion. The court fined Exxon Corporation $150 million, the largest environmental fine ever assessed. All but $25 million was forgiven in recognition of Exxon's expenditures on clean up. Those stretched over four summers, and exceeded $2.1 billion. After four years, the beaches were not clean, but were not cleanable to any further extent. In addition, Exxon paid a criminal penalty of $100 million as restitution for killed fish, birds, sea mammals, and other animal life, and for lands in the region. The state and federal governments split the restitution award. Finally, the corporation paid $900 million over a ten-year period to resolve the civil suit. That money was expended on restoration by the joint federal/state *Exxon Valdez* Oil Spill Trustee Council. Alaska fishers and Natives also filed a class action suit for damages to their livelihood. The district court awarded the plaintiffs $5 billion. The Exxon Corporation has appealed the award, which is yet to be settled.

The disaster led to immediate new federal and state oil spill response legislation. The most significant addition was a requirement that all tankers moving in and out of Alaska be double-hulled by 2015. Other provisions mandated that tankers be accompanied by tugs through Valdez Arm, and that the Coast Guard establish a radar system to monitor them all across the seventy miles of the Sound. Many of these provisions had been recommended in 1973 by the Alaska Pipeline Commission, which had been established to oversee pipeline operation planning and the shipment of the oil from Valdez port. In 1990, the group had been re-formed as the Alaska Oil Spill Commission. Chairman Walter Parker wrote the final report on the *Exxon Valdez* spill, which was scathing in its assignment of responsibility to the oil industry. The disaster could have been prevented, wrote Parker, "by an advanced oil transportation system . . . if Alaskans, state and federal governments, the oil industry and the American public had insisted on stringent safeguards."

The *Exxon Valdez* debacle manifested Alaska's paradoxical relationship with the oil economy to the rest of the nation as nothing had previously. The disaster became overnight, and remains, a symbol of corporate greed and irresponsibility, and of the danger to the environment represented by exploitation and extraction technologies. It is much more difficult now to claim that such technologies are safe. But as Americans viewed the spill as a tragedy, it became an overnight boom for Alaskans. The clean up began almost immediately. Valdez turned into a new, frenetic boomtown. After the executive committee of the Exxon Corporation and all their minions and lawyers arrived to take up all the desirable hotel space and issue daily briefings, the national press crowded in. At the same time state officials from a dozen departments arrived, not the least, lawyers from the Attorney General's office. U.S. Coast Guard personnel were close behind. At the same time, oil spill response equipment began to arrive and be dispersed, though it was essentially useless by this time. Soon, sensing a new boom, Alaskans descended on the community, eager for clean-up jobs. And they were not disappointed. Within two weeks Valdez again regained all of the raw and boisterous character it had embraced during construction of the Alaska pipeline, and before that, during construction of the Copper River and Northwestern Railroad soon after the beginning of the century. Fishers were in particularly high demand, since hundreds of boats were needed to take clean-up personnel and equipment to every cove and island in the oil's path. The money made was handsome, often $1,800 a week, though of small consolation to the fishermen whose long-term livelihood was in jeopardy. Exxon spent most of the $2.1 billion of clean-up costs in Valdez.

Newspapers kept the disaster before the national public for days. In Alaska, the three major newspapers carried at least one story on the spill each day for two months. In addition to the question of Captain Hazelwood's drunkenness, the stories focused on corporate greed, manifest in the corporation's failure to honor the spill response plan, and on government neglect and complacency. One effect of the intense coverage was to fix the disaster firmly in public memory. Another likely impact was on oil legislation pending in the Alaska legislature.

Much analysis in the press focused on early attempts by Exxon Corporation to minimize the magnitude of the spill, and to blame the consortium that operated the pipeline for the disaster. Exxon also blamed the state Department of Environmental Protection for improperly monitoring the industry's oil response readiness. The press campaign was so persistent, aggressive, and detailed that Exxon soon accepted responsibility. But the symbolism of the *Exxon Valdez* spill was weak, both nationally and in Alaska. Exxon reported receiving thousands of returned credit cards. But there was little discussion of reducing oil consumption as a way of minimizing the impact on ecological systems from oil production, transportation, processing and distribution, or exploration. As one commentator quipped, many people mailed in their credit cards, but they drove to the post office to send the letter. Some went deeper. "The economics of how we make our living," former political science professor Charles Konigsberg wrote, cannot be separated "from the health and integrity of the natural world." Nor did Exxon, Alyeska Pipeline Service Company, or the oil industry collectively "have any right to the power they have so arrogantly assumed and exercised over our lives under the mythic cloak of economic separability and priority." Alaskans must learn to distinguish between power and life, Konigsberg pleaded. Only when Alaskans understood "the extent to which myth and language can give illegitimate power to those who wish to control others" could Alaskans begin to take back that power, their power, and use it for "the maintenance of cultural and ecological integrity" in a democratic context. But few Alaskans were as thoughtful and forthright. Most simply decried the spill, and soon slipped comfortably back into the assumptions they had made all along about oil and Alaska: that their personal economics were married to those of the industry, and that the state or someone would protect their marriage.

They were encouraged in such assumptions by a spate of industry-sponsored newspaper ads and by commentary from industry friends. The dominant themes were caution and confidence, but the subtext was unmistakable: fear. The industry feared that new, tighter environmental legislation and new taxes to support the new regulations would erode profits. A full-page ad sponsored by forty-four businesses and the Resource Council for Alaska, Inc., a pro-development association, laid out the argument in unabashed terms. "The tide of emotion over the Prince William Sound oil spill has been running high," the text read. It was "threatening Alaskans with a whole new disaster—an economic one." The governor had a responsibility to demonstrate "real leadership," the sponsors asserted. Alaska needed protection for its environment, "but we also need a strong economy so people can continue to live in this great state." Irresponsible legislation could "drive industry from Alaska and send us backwards into a recession." The sponsors reminded Alaskans that "oil provides more than 80 percent of the state's money—money for schools, permanent fund dividends, community centers, longevity bonuses (annual payments from the state to all persons over 65 years of age) and the basic support of state government." What was needed, the ad proclaimed, was "cool heads and careful action." The sponsors did not include any of the major oil companies, though most of the chief oil field supply companies were listed; rather, they were a cross-section of Alaska's principal businesses, including insurance companies, automobile dealerships, general construction companies, freight companies, an office supply company, and a travel agency. The ad was a particularly transparent and literal form of scare tactics, reminding Alaskans of their dependence on the oil industry. On the same day as the ad was published, the president of the state chamber of commerce published an opinion piece arguing that "punishment" of the oil industry would compound the tragedy. He insisted that the grounding was an accident, and that the shipping companies otherwise had an exemplary safety record. He also reminded Alaskans that their jobs, and their permanent fund dividend checks, were paid for by the industry. The industry must not be "crippled," he wrote. The president of VECO, the largest oil-field supply company, held his own press conference to attack the legislature for a series of new laws under review to tighten spill response requirements, mandate the positioning of clean-up equipment, and provide for frequent inspections and monitoring. The legislative package would "eliminate the industry," he said. He compared the spill to the 1964 earthquake, saying that after that tragedy people had not stood about assessing blame, but had got busy to repair the damage. VECO had just signed a lucrative, long-term contract with Exxon to provide clean-up services. State officials reacted angrily. The commissioner of revenue called the earthquake comparison "absolutely ridiculous." "I think the days when this propaganda and these sort of lies used to work is over with . . . Alaskans have been lied to too many times," he said But the commissioner may have been too sanguine. Although the legislature passed some of the package, more stringent measures were left on the table after hastily called caucuses and committee meetings. A long-time aide of former Governor Hickel summed up the industry position: the state's oil was too important, he said, for an "unsound decision" in response to the Exxon spill.

Despite the clean-up activity and ongoing news reports, for most Alaskans it was back to business as usual soon enough. Throughout the summer, television ads proclaiming the oil industry's "sensitivity to the environment" and to "community values" became standard fare in Alaska programming. Other ads by an in-state industry group, the Alaska Oil and Gas Association repeatedly reminded Alaskans that 85 percent of state general fund revenue came from taxation on industry production. Within months the state's Washington lobbyists were working with industry lawyers to attempt to persuade the first Bush administration to open the Arctic National Wildlife Refuge to oil drilling. The state seemed schizophrenic, prosecuting Exxon and Hazelwood with one hand, calling for more oil exploration and development on the other.

Alaskans clearly were of two minds: they wanted to punish the industry for its breach of trust, but not to do so in such a way as to cause irreparable offense. That schizophrenia was particularly evident in the state legislature, where argument already had raged vigorously for two years over a tax measure highly favorable to the oil industry, the ELF, i.e., the Economic Limit Factor. This was a tax incentive to encourage oil companies to maintain production in small, marginal oil fields. As adopted in 1977, it applied a lower tax to the smaller fields. In 1981, as oil revenues approached their highest levels, under heavy industry lobbying, the legislature agreed to apply the lower tax to the major producing fields (Prudhoe and Kuparuk) as well, to take effect in 1987, when production was estimated to peak. The Alaska Senate comprises just twenty members, so the votes of eleven can pass or reject any piece of legislation. In 1977, the industry spread its political contributions broadly among Senate candidates, targeting tight races, and contributing to opposing candidates.

By 1987, creative and expensive advances in industry technology, primarily reinjection of natural gas, had increased the life of the fields, and put off the peak of production to 1991. In the wake of the 1985-86 downturn in both oil prices and the Alaska economy, some legislators suggested that the ELF should be put off until after the peak of production. Again, heavy lobbying by the industry was successful in maintaining the lower tax on the biggest fields through 1987, 1988, and into 1989.

At that time, the industry threatened that if the lower tax were removed, smaller fields then in line for production definitely would not be developed. An ARCO Alaska vice president said a return to the higher tax rate would hurt individual Alaskans in the long run because it would mean less oil field production. News analysts, on the other hand, interviewed financial experts nationwide who suggested that the impact of raising the tax to previous levels on the productive fields would have little effect on company plans for exploration and development. Governor Cowper supported restoring the tax, and lobbied hard for it. The industry quickly labeled him a "tax and spend liberal." The editor of the conservative *Anchorage Times* accused Cowper of trying to "hoodwink Alaskans into supporting bigger and more costly government operations." A tense rhetorical battle, with implications for campaign finance contributions, was being waged over the ELF when the *Exxon Valdez* went on Bligh Reef.

Some political analysts expected the legislature to quickly revise the ELF to once again apply only to marginal fields, and to take effect after peak production was reached, and legislation was introduced to that effect. But the battle only became more intense. The bill passed in the House, and came to a climactic Senate vote in May. On a Sunday near the end of the session, the senators voted 9–11 to maintain the lower tax that had become effective in 1987. At least one senator immediately filed notice of reconsideration of the vote, for the following day, a normal procedure, though few votes are ever changed on reconsideration. But, on Monday, May 8, two senators changed their votes, and the revised, final vote, was 11–9 for the bill. As a result, the lowered tax was cancelled until the peak of production would be reached, 1991, and was limited to truly marginal fields

The industry had nearly succeeded in controlling the politics of the ELF; without the added pressure of the oil spill, the attempt to revise the tax would surely have failed. In the two years the ELF was in place on Prudhoe and Kuparuk, 1987 and 1988, the state lost about $185 million in tax revenue. In their analysis of oil industry influence in Alaska, political scientists Gerald McBeath and Thomas Morehouse concluded that the industry's reach is extensive, but limited. They note that Alaska is different from other oil-producing states. In Alaska, the oil-producing lands are owned by the state, and all of the North Slope production wells are operated by a small number of companies. Because the state is the owner of the fields, oil industry executives deal with only a small number of highly visible state officials, and those state officials are confronted by only a few owners. The oil service industry is small in comparison to this constituency in states such as Texas and Oklahoma, thus limiting the industry's direct reach in Alaska. State politics are relatively open, and visible. But open politics does not mean immunity from industry pressure. The top ten lobbying spenders include the major industry players. In 1999, BP Exploration (Alaska) spent $300,000, more than any other business; Exxon Corporation was close behind at $280,000, and ARCO spent $269,000.

In addition, the state Department of Revenue and the Department of Law maintain close scrutiny over the industry's tax liability and the revenue stream. The state carried on an eighteen-year tax suit against the oil industry from the beginning of oil flow in the trans-Alaska pipeline. State statute declares that one-eighth of the oil and gas from its lands belongs to the state as a royalty. The state sells that oil to the oil industry, which transports and sells it for the state. The state charged the industry with undervaluing the state's royalty oil, thus cheating it of owed revenue and in 1989 filed claims against fifteen owner companies. One company, Amerada Hess, settled with the state for $319 million. The following year voters amended the state constitution to create a budget reserve fund, called popularly the Constitutional Budget Reserve (CBR), to receive that award, and anticipated future awards from the case. In 1995 the remaining companies settled just as the case was finally to go to trial. The state gained about $1 billion from the settlement.

⋈ ⋈

The societal reach of the oil industry in Alaska was greater than its political reach. Within the state the industry was pervasive. Radio and television ads, daily news, and visual cues across the landscape, from office towers in downtown Anchorage to the pipeline snaking through the wilderness, to tanker traffic in Prince William Sound and in Cook Inlet—all reminded the populace of oil's importance, and their dependency. The Alaska legislature probably represented Alaskans' ambivalence toward the industry following the *Exxon Valdez* disaster. An important aspect of Big Oil's transformation of Alaska was a change in the historical antipathy toward absentee investors in the region's resources. More dependent than ever on such investment, Alaskans found it more difficult to position themselves against it. Increasingly, the term "partner" was used to describe the relationship. The annual dividends paid by the Alaska Permanent Fund strengthened that sense of partnership, but in a manner that included a certain perversity, as the final chapter reveals.

7

Dividend Alaska

༽༽ ༼

As Alaskans approached the new millennium they found their society riven by the same tensions that had characterized it throughout the twentieth century. The most pronounced oppositions were still those between Alaskans and traditional "others," with whom they seemed locked in a steely, mutually frigid embrace. Viewing themselves as modern pioneers on the "last frontier," committed to the establishment and enjoyment of modern material culture, most non–Native Alaskans fiercely resented federal exercises of sovereignty that constrained their sense of rightful autonomy. Even more, they bristled at national and local environmentalists who worked to preserve Alaska's wilderness areas from mineral and petroleum exploration and development, and from encroaching urbanization. At the same time, they often seemed incognizant of the impact of their actions on Alaska's Native people, who felt just as strongly their own right to autonomy, their own right to full participation in modern American culture, and their commitment to traditional wilderness access. To these familiar oppositions, which had become almost second nature, Alaskans added a new tension, or rather an ancient one in new garb: jealous lust for the money the state handed to them every October as their portion of the spoils of the exploitation of their natural resources, exploitation on which they depended directly for the opportunity to be Alaskans at all.

Despite the battles over authorization of the Alaska pipeline, the Native claims settlement act and the Alaska lands act, and the crises of the 1980s, most particularly the economic crash associated with falling oil prices and the tragedy of the *Exxon Valdez* oil spill, most Alaskans seemed only dimly to perceive the external forces that guided their lives. Their circumstances reflected real political and economic conditions, and they responded to each new challenge with vigor and determination. But they seemed suspended beyond time in the manner of their responses. The language, the rhetoric, and the ideas were timeless.

Governor Walter Hickel captured the essence of Alaskan resentment in his 1990 election campaign. Alaska, he said, must become an "owner state." Though his attempts to define the term remained elusive, he seemed to mean that Alaska should use its power as owner of the state's natural resources, and the wealth derived from that ownership, to establish a more stable state economy. One way to do that, Hickel insisted, would be to spend state funds to diversify the economy. But the term had much more utility as a political mantra than it did as a carefully conceived program of economic development. It conjured up images of power, control, and independence. And it presented a pugnacious stance to any who would trespass.

Elected governor a second time in 1990, Hickel applied his notion of trespass in an imaginative suit against the federal government in the U.S. Court of Federal Claims. The inspiration for the suit was the "sagebrush rebellion" of the early 1980s. As noted earlier, this was a protest by users of the public lands in western states against new environmental legislation that limited access and exploitation of those lands. Much of the legal language of the sagebrush rebellion and Hickel's suit came from the Mountain States Legal Foundation of Denver, Colorado, headed by James Watt before his appointment as Interior Secretary in the Reagan administration. The suit charged the U.S. Congress with violating its sacred "compact" with Alaskans, the statehood act, which granted the state 104 million acres of land and provided that 90 percent of federal mineral lease revenue collected in the state would be passed on to the state to help pay its administrative costs. The suit charged that by passing the claims settlement act (ANCSA) and the Alaska lands act (ANILCA), Congress had eliminated leasing, and thus leasing revenue, from the 44 million and 104 million acres taken. The attorneys calculated the lost revenue to the state at the time of the suit to be $29 billion.

Despite the protestations of the attorney who assembled the suit, the state attorney general, and the Mountain States Legal Foundation, the case had no chance of success. It was based on the idea that the Congress could not constitutionally change the terms of the statehood act without the consent of the people of Alaska. Alaskans had voted in 1958 to accept the statehood act, and in that action, the state's attorneys charged, had made it an unbreakable compact. Constitutional experts across the country, queried by the editor of the *Anchorage Daily News*, thought the case ludicrous. The issues of federal sovereignty over the states, of Congress's right and need to change existing legislation to meet changed constituent demands and perceptions, and of the constitutionality of federal ownership and management of public lands had all been upheld by the U.S. Supreme Court many times over.

In 1996 the State of Alaska and the United States presented their arguments in court. The federal judge dismissed the suit in short order. There is no such thing as a binding statehood compact, the judge asserted. Only those parts of such an act are irrevocable which the parties state explicitly are such upon passage of the act. The federal lease revenue provisions of the act were not so identified in 1958, the judge ruled, nor were they singled out in the plebiscite. "Ultimately," the judge wrote,

> *the subject matter of the Statehood Act—entry into a union of states—is* sui generis *and cannot be strictly compressed into a contractual or legislative mode. . . . The statehood debate cannot be analogized to the normal negotiations between parties to commercial contracts.*

The state appealed to the Court of Appeals for the District of Columbia. The court dismissed the suit with a terse statement "Judge Bruggink's opinion is thoroughly supported with cited and quoted authority and record evidence. Nothing more needs to be said." Finally, in 1998, the U.S. Supreme Court declined to hear the state's further appeal.

For Hickel, the issue had never been the money. It was the frontier. The state should be free to develop whatever land it could, Hickel believed, and in ANCSA and ANILCA Congress had reduced the state's ability to do that. In doing so, Hickel was convinced it had broken a solemn promise. So persuaded was he that while the suit was pending, he directed the state office of public information to produce a video about the suit, *Broken Promises,* at a cost of $30,000, which was distributed to schools statewide. It told the story of a perfidious Congress that callously broke the solemn compact with Alaska's people. Because of his credibility with Alaskans, Hickel did significant damage with the lawsuit and the video. Because of the oppositional mode of thinking so common in Alaska, many Alaskans, including many politicians, accepted Hickel's assertions as truth. The theme of broken promises was used repeatedly in political campaigns and in political discourse on federal/state issues critical to Alaska. The federal government had an obligation to develop its lands in Alaska, meaning opening them to mineral exploration and development, the state's lawyers charged, and did not do so. The broken promises theme was another way of stating that the state's rights had been repeatedly violated by the federal government, the paradigm of Ernest Gruening's history of Alaska published before statehood, and of the statehood campaign itself. Alaskan politicians seem to have found no other patriotic mantra to parade before voters to generate votes and support.

The states' rights theme was used inappropriately in the conflict over rural subsistence rights and access. Subsistence became a highly charged, highly visible, and strongly emotional issue in Alaska. It dominated much political discourse in the 1990s. ANILCA guaranteed traditional subsistence utilization of federal lands, including conservation units, as we have seen, and access across federal lands for those purposes. The act required the state to recognize and enforce a subsistence preference for rural Alaskans. A racial preference would be unconstitutional, so the language of the act is "rural preference." There are non-Native subsistence users in wilderness Alaska, and their access is likewise guaranteed. But most subsistence users in Alaska are Native. Subsistence is therefore primarily, but not exclusively, a Native issue. But it is also an urban issue, for many urban residents claim a cultural attachment to hunting and fishing, even if the activity is not for subsistence, but for sport and recreation.

The rural preference in ANILCA is in conflict with the state constitution, which declares that Alaska's natural resources belong equally to all citizens. Nonetheless, in 1978 the Alaska legislature passed a law providing a subsistence preference for "customary and traditional uses . . . for direct personal or family consumption, and for customary trade, barter or sharing." In 1985, the state Supreme Court struck down that law. The legislature responded with a law establishing a rural preference for persons residing in the area where the subsistence activity took place. This, too, the state Supreme Court disallowed. Called by Governor Cowper to a special session in 1990, the state House failed to pass a state constitutional amendment on the issue by a single vote.

At statehood, all states in the union assumed management of fish and game resources on federal lands in their states, unless the lands were managed by special legislation, such as in national parks. ANILCA

Katie John, Athabaskan elder who sued successfully for subsistence rights on navigable waters in Alaska, at Copper River.
(Courtesy Anchorage Daily News, photograph by Erik Hill)

mandated that the state's failure to recognize the subsistence preference on federal lands would lead to federal management of fish and game resources on federal land in Alaska, and on state lands used by game and other resources using federal land. With the state out of compliance with ANILCA, the federal government assumed management of subsistence hunting on federal lands, which it retains to this day. The state could be brought into compliance with the ANILCA preference by passage of a constitutional amendment, but the legislature, invariably invoking the rhetoric of states' rights, has refused to pass such an amendment, even though polls in the state have repeatedly shown that Alaskan voters favor it.

In January 1998, the Alaska Legislative Council, at the request of several conservative members of the legislature, filed a suit challenging the federal government's authority to preempt state management of fish and game. Attorneys' fees were $175,000. This was a simple states' rights suit; it was symbolic, and had no chance of success. But it provided legislators with an opportunity once again for patriotic posturing. A federal judge dismissed the suit soon after it was filed.

In the wilderness regions and on the conservation units, federal resource management boards allocate subsistence quotas and arrange access with little or no difficulty. Native and non–Native subsistence users and game wardens for the most part easily agree on such matters, for the patterns of use are long established. Natives were offended by the use of state funds to fight for states' rights at the expense, it seemed to them, of their traditional activities and the security of the resources they depended upon.

Native discomfiture turned to anger over the issue of Native sovereignty. In 1993 President Clinton recognized 227 Native tribes in Alaska, for most their first federal recognition as tribes, qualifying them for federal tribal benefits. But questions about tribal status in Alaska had lingered since passage of the claims settlement act in 1971, and remained after 1993 because of the lack of reservations in the state. The settlement act had been broadly interpreted to extinguish Indian Country in Alaska. While that did not affect the sovereignty of tribal governments, which exist in most villages, it did limit that sovereignty to internal tribal matters, unlike tribal sovereignty on Indian reservations in the lower forty-eight states, which is broad and far-reaching. The act extinguished the two reservations successfully created by the Interior Department in the 1940s. The lands of the former reservations, 1.8 million acres, went to the new regional corporation. The inhabitants of the only two villages on the former Venetie reservation, Venetie and Arctic Village, turned the new corporation lands back to the tribal governments, who thought this action displaced the state's power to tax and regulate activities on their lands. They believed they had the same level of sovereignty as other tribal governments in the United States, and hoped that this expanded sovereignty would give them direct control, especially over economic development and alcohol regulation. The tribal government levied a tax on a contractor building a village school. The state sued to confirm that Indian Country did not exist in Alaska (at least in this case), that the state's authority was not diminished, and that the tribe's sovereignty was limited to internal matters.

At the district court level, the state won, but in 1996 the Ninth Circuit Court of Appeals found for the tribe. The ruling touched off new enthusiasm in parts of rural Alaska for tribal governance. The state immediately appealed to the U.S. Supreme Court, and the legislature appropriated $1 million to pursue the case. Many Alaska Natives interpreted the state's eagerness to fight tribal sovereignty as further evidence that the state did not honor their unique conditions and their right to sovereignty. When coupled with the legislature's refusal to adopt and send to the voters a constitutional amendment guaranteeing a rural subsistence preference, Native leaders concluded that legislative leaders had turned their backs on Native people. The U.S. Supreme Court ruled in February 1998, that ANCSA had extinguished Indian Country, and that the tribal government did not have the power of taxation over external affairs on its lands. The decision dashed their raised hopes, and left many Natives feeling diminished. The feeling was exacerbated when the state legislature changed the funding formula for rural schools in 1998. The new formula transferred a portion of annual state education funding from rural districts, which were losing population, to urban districts, where the population was growing.

Hopes had been growing in Native Alaska throughout the decade. In 1994 a joint federal/state commission on Native conditions, the Alaska Natives Commission, had made a series of forward-looking recommendations to improve Native life in Alaska. Congress had created the commission in response to recommendations made in a special Alaska Federation of Natives report published in 1989. Titled *The AFN Report on the Status of Alaska Natives: A Call for Action*, the frank and stark report detailed rates of teen suicide and child abuse, infectious disease, lack of educational attainment, and lack of economic prospects for many villages. Though not as disheartening as the 1968 Federal Field Committee survey, the report explained clearly there was more work to be done. The members of the Alaska Natives Commission were conservative in outlook, appointed by President George Bush and by Alaska Governor Walter Hickel. The commission published its findings in July 1994. They were familiar, but the recommendations were not.

First, the commissioners asked Alaska's non-Native majority to hear and respond to Natives' need for greater self-determination. Unlike Native Americans in the lower forty-eight states, at the time most tribes in Alaska were not formally recognized. The commission said that the state should reverse its long-standing policy and legally recognize the widespread presence of tribes in Alaska. Both the state and federal governments should use tribal and other Native institutions to design and deliver services to Natives, the commissioners recommended, particularly in the areas of substance abuse, health, and subsistence. Further, the state should cooperate with tribal governments and tribal courts to improve law enforcement in rural areas. Federal law should let Native corporations transfer their lands to tribal governments or other Native entities. Congress should rewrite all laws that suggest Alaska Natives do not enjoy the powers of self-government accorded Indians in the lower forty-eight states. Congress should repeal the part of the Native claims settlement act that extinguished any claims to aboriginal hunting and fishing rights. The existing, limited Native hiring preference should be expanded to cover all federal programs serving Alaska Natives.

These recommendations generated considerable optimism in Native Alaska. They called for a new relationship between the state and tribal entities, and for a new level of understanding among Alaska's people. In the face of this optimism, the legislature's failure to address subsistence, its decision to fight expanded Native sovereignty, and its adjustment of the education funding formula came as serious blows. In May 1999, one of the state's most respected Native leaders, Byron Mallott, former president of Sealaska Corporation and of the AFN, and at the time executive director of the Alaska Permanent Fund Corporation, published an opinion piece in the *Anchorage Daily News* in which he wrote, "It's not a good time to be a Native Alaskan." "What is being heard and seen by Native people is a cacophony of negatives and meanness," he said, "emanating largely from the Legislature, but echoed in many places." Subsistence, sovereignty, and education were not the real issue. "What is the issue is the sour and vile residue of the debate itself." It had, he said, "opened the eyes of Native Alaskans to what may portend their place in Alaska's future if current trends prevail." That future was one that would allow "public policy and programs to be developed without our real participation and to move in directions that marginalize our existence and are not responsive to our circumstances."

The words were harsh, but they apparently carried the sentiments of many. Several weeks later, a state commission appointed by Governor Tony Knowles in February 1998, the Commission on Rural Governance and Empowerment, published a report of its eighteen-month study of Native affairs. Alaska had reached a "crisis point," the commission reported, as rural villages "give up on the state and look for solutions in their role as federally recognized tribes." While many Alaskans distrust the federal government, the report said, "rural residents tend to regard the state government as cold, distant, hidden, uninformed about life at the local level and controlled by somebody else." A "massive political rift" had been growing between urban and rural Alaska, the report noted. The commission recommended dialogue and education to promote a "healing process." Other leaders confirmed the Rural Governance commission's finding. One of the AFN's founders called on Natives to band together as a constituency to effect a change in the composition of the legislature.

The tension generated by Mallott's opinion piece and by the Rural Governance commission report was felt throughout both urban and village Alaska. Soon leadership organizations, including Commonwealth North, the state humanities council, and the Anchorage Chamber of Commerce, began discussions on the "urban/rural split" in the state. Church groups began to invite Native leaders to address the sources of distrust, and to help establish education programs for members. The United Way established a task force to address the issue. And Governor Tony Knowles took two steps to greatly increase the potential for meaningful discourse on the nature of Alaskan culture. First, in September 2000, he signed an administrative order by which the state formally recognized the 227 federally recognized tribes in the state. "Alaska's tribes are alive and well in this new millennium, just as they have been for the untold millennia past," the governor said. "It is time to embrace tribal governments as partners in the future of this great state. It is time to move on as friends." Then, in December 2000, the governor established the Alaska Inter-Tribal Council, comprising twelve state cabinet officers and forty-six tribal representative to work on a government-to-government basis to address Native needs in justice, policing, health, education, economic viability, material infrastructure, and other challenges facing village Alaska. Further, in August 2001 the governor convened a select leadership panel on subsistence that recognized a fundamental link between Native culture and subsistence use of resources.

All of these measures helped to address the sources of distrust between Native and non-Native Alaskans. Yet massive problems remained. The state continued to be out of compliance with federal mandates on subsistence. Education funding for village schools still rankled Native leaders and educators. Village economic sustainability remained a pervasive and formidable hurdle. The future remained unsettled and uncertain.

☻ ☻

In August 2000, officials in the National Park Service in Alaska, the Alaska Conservation Foundation, and the University of Alaska Anchorage invited former President Jimmy Carter and Interior Secretary Cecil Andrus to Alaska to help commemorate the twentieth anniversary of the passage of the Alaska lands act, ANILCA, by Congress. While in the state, Carter addressed the Alaska Conservation Foundation, recently a new partner of David Rockefeller Jr.'s Alaska Fund for the Future, including some remarks about the history of the Alaska lands bill. Carter had said a number of times in the years after his presidency that ANILCA was one of the things he was proudest of. At the luncheon he said that there were some things not in the act that he wished had been included, among them better protection for the 19-million-acre Arctic National Wildlife Refuge (ANWR).

To correct that perceived omission in prepared remarks, Carter called on President Clinton to give the refuge monument status before he left office. That would effectively prevent oil drilling there into the foreseeable future, Carter said, because although Congress had the power to do so, it had never yet rescinded monument status given by a president to any public lands. ANILCA expanded the boundaries of ANWR, and designated 8 million acres of the refuge as wilderness. The 1.8-million acre coastal plain (8 percent of the total refuge area), adjacent to the state's Prudhoe Bay and associated deposits, was established in the act as a study area. The act authorized the Secretary of the Interior to determine the likelihood of economic oil deposits under the plain. Several studies have yielded a number of estimates, the most optimistic being a 46 percent chance, very high by industry standards. The median estimate of how much oil might be found is 10 billion barrels. Some industry geologists have said there may be 16 billion barrels. ANILCA provided that Congress would make the final determination on whether or not to open the coastal plain, called the "1002 area" after the section of the act in which the mandate appears.

Carter's call for monument status for the refuge set off a storm of protest in Alaska. Governor Tony Knowles, scheduled to appear at the university to introduce the participants in a panel discussion, boycotted the event. Instead, he released at a press conference a strong, some said rude, others scathing, letter to Carter. "You are wrong," Knowles told the former president, "to dismiss the role of the Coast Plain . . ." as a remedy for high crude oil and gasoline prices, the development of which could create "hundreds of thousands of jobs across the nation. You are wrong ignoring the pressing needs of Alaska's Native families . . . whose hopes are nourished by the jobs, education, and decent quality of life that oil and gas development has a will bring to their children." "You are wrong," Knowles continued, "in calling for executive action at the midnight hour instead of an open, public democratic process of carefully weighting values in the light of day." Finally, "you are wrong to call upon the President to take an illegal action that is prohibited by ANILCA." In this last, Knowles referred to the clause of the act that prohibits the withdrawal of any new conservation units in Alaska larger than five thousand acres. Alaskans understood better than most Americans the necessity of maintaining the health of the land, Knowles wrote. "At the same time, we do not fear developing the resources found within it. As we have done in the North Slope oil fields, we can develop the resources of ANWR . . . while protecting our environment."

ANWR was the most controversial environmental issue in Alaska at the end of the twentieth century. Knowles' strong letter to Carter captured well the frontier assumptions and convictions of the majority of Alaskans, and their failure to appreciate the essence of modern environmentalism. He dismissed by omission the environmental idea that the future of wilderness demands the end of development on some parts of the public lands legacy of the nation. At the same time, he implied that the best use of those lands is economic development. He used the classic language of "wise use," language most Americans would understand well. He was somewhat disingenuous in implying that Native people support the opening of the refuge; Gwitchin people on the Venetie and Arctic Village lands just south of the refuge do not, though the Eskimos of the North Slope, whose local government encompasses Prudhoe Bay and the northern end of the Alaska pipeline, do. But Knowles carried majority opinion in Alaska with him in his expression of sentiments on ANWR, if not approval of the tone of his response. For the majority of Alaskans, environmentalism had not altered their embrace of the wilderness paradigm. They were in the state to develop its resources for their profit, and the nation's.

Development-minded Alaskans singled out the National Park Service for particular abuse on environmental issues. Most of the fifty million acres of Alaska wilderness designated by ANILCA are managed by the Park Service, though an appreciable number of acres are managed by the Fish and Wildlife Service. For miners, especially, the NPS was a thorn. The thrust of criticism was that in implementation of the act, Park Service personnel did not appreciate how different the rules governing Alaskan conservation units were from those in the lower forty-eight states. In the latter parks and refuges, hunting is not allowed, "traditional uses" such as motorized access to subsistence resources are banned, and mining is prohibited. All of these uses were permitted in Alaska, and critics charged that new managers coming to Alaska from other parts of the NPS system were not familiar with the Alaska exceptions, and instead managed the units by the more restrictive standards. Section 101(b) of ANILCA states that the act is sufficient protection for Alaska's conservation resources, and therefore the need for future legislation is obviated. Critics charged that unit managers used ANILCA as a beginning for tightening access to resources. Given the finality announced in the act, critics saw no need for further management studies. Critics acknowledged that the Native access guaranteed in the act had been honored by unit managers, but complained that the attitude of NPS, Fish and Wildlife Service, and Bureau of Land Management field personnel was often contentious. Title XI of ANILCA provided for a transportation utility system; critics charged no such system had been developed. They asserted that unit managers discouraged motorized access, guaranteed in the act. Many argued that helicopters were to be included in the motorized access; the NPS prohibited helicopters. In the Kantishna area of Denali Park, existing mining claims were to be protected, though current environmental regulations and safeguards were to be observed. NPS managers in Denali denied operating permits to miners on environmental grounds. In recommendations for implementation, executive director of the Alaska Miners' Association Steve Borrell called for "removing restrictive conservation designations from some of the lands now in the conservation system units," in other words, for revisiting the act itself.

Loggers reacted similarly to the implementation of ANILCA, the Tongass Timber Reform Act, and the land use plan developed by the Forest Service. The closure of the pulp mills in 1993 and 1997 reduced the demand for pulp timber, but there was still a market for the export of logs to Japan and under congressional legislation the Forest Service contracts called for squaring the logs into shunts before shipment, a value-added provision to generate jobs. Loggers charged that the fifteen hundred jobs lost in the forest products industry in the decade were due to timber harvest cutbacks mandated by the reform act and implemented by the Forest Service. But the Forest Service had not been able to find buyers for the leases it put up for bid. Primarily, this was because Native corporations, as private land holders, could ship raw, uncut logs, for which there was a substantial market in Japan. Native corporations harvested the 550,000 acres of Native land in the forest aggressively through the 1990s. Of 567 million board feet of timber cut on forested lands in Southeast in 1999, 465 million were cut by Native corporations, almost all of it for the export market.

After the reform act and the mill closures, the Forest Service was in a much better position to manage the forest for wise use. By 2000, vast swaths of the forest had been clear cut. The density of new growth on older clear cuts restricted sunlight, so that the forest floor produced little forage for Sitka and black tail deer, which had been common before the intense harvest. Many salmon streams were inundated by sloughing of their banks, silting from erosion and skidding logs, and from lack of buffers left on their banks. State biologists called it a desert landscape, and worried whether the forest could renew itself. "It looks like hell," acknowledged former Sealaska chief executive Byron Mallott. "We can make some harsh judgments now, but it was done under the existing regulations." And the money that logging generated transformed some shareholders' lives for the better, he said. Across Alaska, Natives insisted on utilizing the resources of their ANCSA lands for the benefit of their shareholders, even if, as in Sealaska's case, it meant despoiling the resource.

The tensions manifest in Alaska's urban/rural divide, in the state's special permutation of states' rights advocacy, in miners' and loggers' protests over conservation area access, and Native corporations' justifications for environmental despoliation punctuated media reports irregularly but persistently. The sense of crisis they generated, however, was overshadowed by two additional issues that broke into Alaska consciousness late in the 1990s that, because of their comprehensive nature, became matters of urgent and consistent attention for all Alaskans. The first was the state budget, rendered severely critical by falling oil prices; the second was consolidation in the oil industry as British Petroleum proposed to purchase ARCO, thereby creating a virtual monopoly on Alaska oil production. Both manifested once again the extraordinary degree of dependency of Alaska's economy on exploitation of the single natural resource: oil. That dependency lurked as a seldom-spoken subtext.

After the price crash in 1985-86, oil prices stabilized at about $20 a barrel. After contraction of the real estate market, housing prices, and state spending, the Alaska economy proved stronger than many economists had expected. Tourism grew substantially, and both Anchorage and Fairbanks international airports became regional redistribution centers for small packages shipped to Asia by air. In 1999 and 2000 the Anchorage airport handled more freight by volume than any airport in the nation. But in late 1997 oil prices began to slide, a function of an economic crisis in East Asia, a series of mild U.S. winters, and decreased world demand. In 1998 princes averaged only $12.50 a barrel. Alaskans began to keep a wary eye on the daily price of Alaska North Slope crude. By the summer of 1999, the price at times dipped below $9 a barrel. The state budget could not be balanced on $9 oil. In 1998 the $6 billion budget faced a revenue shortfall of $600 million. In 1999 it would be $1 billion. The conservative state legislature repeatedly cut spending, but soon reached the limit of cuts the public would tolerate. In 1995 legislators began to balance the budget by transferring funds from the Budget Reserve Fund, known popularly as the Constitutional Budget Reserve (CBR), established by voters in 1990. The legislature had placed additional windfall revenues in the CBR, which is managed, like the Alaska Permanent Fund, as an investment account, and by 1998 the account held $3 billion. That fund could be sustained while making up budget shortfalls of several hundred thousand dollars, but obviously would be unsustainable at shortfalls of $1 billion.

Governor Tony Knowles convened a blue-ribbon panel of Alaska economists, financial and business leaders, politicians, and civic spokespersons to address what had become popularly known as the "fiscal gap." News about the fiscal gap had begun to permeate Alaskan consciousness. People who had lived through the 1985–86 crash and exodus manifested acute anxiety whenever the "gap" was mentioned, not unlike that observed in survivors of the 1964 Great Alaska Earthquake whenever a particularly strong tremor shook the region ever afterward. The task force recommended a package of modest budget cuts and new taxes, particularly reinstitution of the state income tax, which had been abolished when the Permanent Fund was created. The governor endorsed the plan and told Alaskans it would provide a "soft landing" for the falling economy. Stalking about the landscape unmentioned, but embarrassingly visible and intrusive, like the emperor with no clothes, was the Alaska Permanent Fund. Established as a public savings account, the Fund stood in 1999 at $26 billion. Yet, no politician dared propose using any of it to close the fiscal gap, for to do so would be political suicide. Voters had become increasingly jealous of the annual distribution of half of the earnings of the Fund to all residents. The task force decided that there was more danger in asking voters to tap the Permanent Fund than in asking them to pay taxes.

But the legislature refused to take up the issue of new taxes, and left Alaska voters with a dilemma that mocked any assertions of civic responsibility: $26 billion in the bank and no way to use it for needed services. In the meantime, education funding suffered at all levels, health and human services were under-funded, and municipalities received less money from the state to pay for such basic services as fire protection and emergency medical response.

In late 1997 and early 1998, the state humanities council held a statewide forum on the Permanent Fund. The council conducted one hundred town meetings in forty communities across the state, including the major urban centers, small towns, and Native villages. Several conclusions emerged from the meetings. Participants did seem to appreciate the paradox of the state having an astronomical savings account but no way to use it except to distribute some of its earnings to individuals. On the other hand, they were clear that they wanted the Fund to be truly permanent. These Alaskans expressed overwhelming support for the dividend program. They also manifested significant distrust of public officials, and concomitantly, noted their appreciation for being listened to in the expression of their opinions. Perhaps surprisingly, they also were nearly unanimous in support for some kind of new taxation.

In 1998 Governor Knowles ran successfully for re-election. In his budget address soon afterward, he introduced an integrated financial plan to achieve state financial stability. The plan would have restored a personal income tax and used $4 billion from the Permanent Fund to offset budget shortfalls. But the plan was dead on arrival in the legislature. Legislators could afford to eschew both new taxes and the use of Permanent Fund principal, and instead talk of more budget trimming, because they knew they could make up the shortfall by using the Budget Reserve. Critics began to wonder aloud at what price it would no longer be cost effective for British Petroleum and ARCO, operators of the North Slope wells and the major investors in Alaska's oil, to continue to produce in Alaska. Officials of the companies said $10 a barrel was the break-even point, but independent analysts suggested that the companies would make profits at any price above $7. 35. Through 1998 and 1999 the companies laid off successive waves of workers and consolidated their Prudhoe Bay management structure, though they each continued to operate separate portions of the North Slope. BP and ARCO both began to curtail exploration and production, and other companies with exploratory leases did the same. In 1998 eighteen exploration rigs drilled on the North Slope; in 1999 eleven of those were stacked, i.e., shut down. State analysts worried that production might slip by 200,000 barrels a day, dropping pipeline flow below 1 million barrels for the first time since start-up in 1977.

Despite these anxieties, however, the Alaska economy was much stronger in 1998-99 than it had been in 1985-86. Though it cut $430 million from its Alaska expenditures in 1999, BP still spent $850 million in the state that year. ARCO undertook a media advertising campaign promising "No Decline After '99." BP continued development on two new fields, Alpine and North Star, and continued to test new technologies for increasing yields. At the same time, federal spending in Alaska continued at record levels, comprising one-third of the total economic base. Also, the Permanent Fund dividend distribution put nearly $1 billion into the economy. People were nervous, but not panicked. Before adjourning in May 1999, legislators called for a special advisory election, scheduled for September 14, to query voters on whether or not to tap the Permanent Fund. The question was poorly worded, and the purpose for which the finds might be used was left unclear. The answer was a resounding "No," 83 percent of voters rejecting the proposition.

Then, as had happened so many times in Alaska's history, the unexpected occurred. OPEC curtailed production, the East Asian economy began to recover, and oil prices began to rise. Throughout 1999 the price rose steadily, reaching about $15 a barrel in July, and $20 a barrel before Christmas. Through 2000 the price averaged very close to $20 most of the year, dropping closer to $15 at year's end. Analysts expected the price to stay stabilized at a figure above $15. The impact was spectacular. BP, which had reported world profits of $6.2 billion in 1999, reported $14.2 billion in 2000. Talk of the fiscal gap and an economic downturn evaporated. The state legislature watched as the gap narrowed daily, and the hard questions of how to develop a long-range fiscal plan for the state could be put off another time.

But the momentary crisis demonstrated once again the fragility of Alaska's economy and its high level of dependence on forces beyond Alaskans' control. That dependence generates insecurity, and motivates Alaskans to support economic development, irrespective of environmental implications. Throughout the 1998-99 price crisis, pro-development forces in the state kept the possibility of opening ANWR before the public. Senator Frank Murkowski was chairman of the Energy and Natural Resources Committee in the 106th Congress, and Rep. Don Young was chair of the Resources Committee in the House. Both used their positions to urge expansion of oil development in Alaska. They applauded heartily when Interior Secretary Bruce Babbitt decided to hold a lease sale on the National Petroleum Reserve – Alaska, along the western border of Alaska's Prudhoe Bay lands. Both also kept up a steady drumbeat of criticism of Forest Service management of the Tongass National Forest. Both were also highly critical of a decision by the National Park Service to close crabbing and to phase out commercial fishing in Glacier Bay National Monument as activities incompatible with the values of parkland. Murkowski, in particular, sought a way to override that decision. In these and other actions the senator and the congressman revealed their devotion to economic development above all other considerations, sharing the orientation of all of their political predecessors.

In April 2000, an event occurred which brought a kind of unity to Alaska history and to analysis of the relationship between environment and culture in the state. At the same time it encompassed virtually all the salient elements—economic, political, and cultural—that define the character of Alaska at the end of the century, and will continue to do so into the foreseeable future. On April 13, the U.S. Federal Trade Commission (FTC) in Washington, D.C., approved a merger of British Petroleum-Amoco and ARCO oil companies. The deal, said Alaska Attorney General Bruce Botelho, would have more effect on Alaska's future than anything that had happened in the past. The *Anchorage Daily News* said that the agreement "sweeps aside twenty-three years of history." The new merger made BP-Amoco-ARCO the third largest oil company worldwide, behind Royal Dutch/Shell and Exxon Mobil. BP-Amoco-ARCO has a world market capitalization of about $200 billion. BP paid about $30 billion for the acquisition of ARCO.

Reaction in Alaska to the new merger was nearly unanimously favorable, though the state had negotiated with the oil companies intensely over the course of the year leading to the final decision. Prior to the merger, BP and ARCO together had controlled about 70 percent of oil production in Alaska. Though the two had cooperated in operation of the North Slope fields, they had remained separate companies. Alaskans feared that the merger would create a virtual monopoly. Governor Tony Knowles worked with executives of the companies to construct an arrangement that met the requisites of state anti-trust laws, and insured competition. He announced the agreement with high promise and fanfare, and the state, BP, and ARCO produced a glossy insert for newspapers in the state explaining the "Charter for Development" with BP and ARCO. It seemed that the merger was well on its way to winning FTC approval.

The legislature, however, found the arrangement too favorable to the industry. Members appointed a Special Committee on Mergers that called for more divestiture of BP's North Slope interest than the governor had.

The FTC also had its own problems with divestiture, and at the eleventh hour, filed suit in federal court to block the merger. FTC officials said the proposed acquisition could lead to significant increases in the price of crude oil for refiners in California and other West Coast states. In addition, they contended that the merged corporation would be able to manipulate crude oil prices.

In difficult negotiations, the oil companies, the state, and the FTC worked out the final arrangement to allow the deal to go ahead with a 5-0 vote of approval from the FTC. The principal feature called upon BP to sell ARCO's North Slope assets within thirty days of the merger. Phillips Petroleum agreed to buy those holdings for about $7 billion. That reduced BP's share of North Slope oil production to about 44 percent; the state's proposal would have reduced BP to a 55 percent share. Phillips gained 32 percent of production, and Exxon retained 21 percent. BP also had to sell a crude oil marketing hub the companies controlled in Oklahoma. BP acquired all of ARCO's other interests in the U.S., South America, Africa, and Indonesia. In addition, BP took over complete management of North Slope oil production, representing an annual savings of about $100 million. The new corporation acquired the rights to a major percentage of North Slope natural gas supplies, increasing its control from 6.4 to 9.2 trillion cubic feet. The company bet that in the future its natural gas share would more than offset what it was giving up in the current share of oil production.

During the negotiations, BP had carried on a vigorous media campaign in Alaska. Richard Campbell, CEO of BP's Alaska arm, BP Exploration (Alaska), promised that the merger would mean more tax revenue and more jobs for Alaskans, over time, because lower operating costs would allow the company to undertake more exploration and ultimately, more production. For weeks the company ran half-page newspaper ads to generate support of the governor's plan, featuring photos of both prominent and unknown Alaskans professing their support of the merger. Then, periodically, they ran ads with many of the same individuals sending the same message collectively. Even the president of Alaska's Special Olympics 2001 organization was drafted into approval.

Economic development was the unabashed message sent by the industry, the governor, and supporters of the merger, economic development on whatever terms could be arranged. A twenty-five-year oil field veteran wrote an opinion piece in which he described his early childhood in Seward, Alaska, contrasting it with the comforts of contemporary life. People lived in small houses no larger than six hundred square feet situated on gravel streets. Many of the homes would not hold much heat at temperatures below freezing. The telephones were on a party line. There was one radio station and a weekly newspaper. Employment was seasonal. People did not go on vacations, and "they did not have expensive toys like snow machines, four wheelers or airplanes. There was no big screen television." The old-timer noted that, "by far the greatest changes came from oil development." What were the benefits? Thousands of year-round, private-sector jobs, improved schools and roads, access to home purchases through the state-owned mortgage corporation, small and large business loans from the state-owned Alaska Industrial Development and Export Authority, Alaska Technology and Science Foundation grants for high-tech development, construction of sports arenas, convention centers, libraries and performing arts centers, and not least, the Alaska Permanent Fund. This was a near-perfect recitation of the dominant Alaskan understanding of reality in modern Alaska. The frontier exists to provide material development for those willing to go there. Reliance on absentee capital and control, even with the insecurity that accompanied it, was a price Alaskans were happy to pay for the material benefit they derived: big houses, snow machines, vacations, schools, convention centers. The writer might have added that the rhetoric and mythology of states' rights and broken promises helped explain the dependence in an acceptable way, and masked the economic and cultural realities of modern Alaskan life.

When former political science professor and social critic Charles Konigsberg read the "Charter for Development," he set out to explain the danger it represented to Alaska and its citizens. The merger had little to do with business economics, he said. It had to do with the power to determine public policy, not only in regard to the extraction of oil, but all of Alaska's natural resources, and everything derived from the extraction. What was at stake, he urged, was the question of how Alaskans should live their lives. The merger represented concentrated economic power, Konigsberg said. And history is replete with the record of the arrogant abuse of such power, undermining the right of the people of a society to determine for themselves the course of their lives, on their own terms. He called upon Alaskans to rise to that opportunity, that responsibility.

The governor and the oil executives had consistently used the term "partners" in Alaska's development, which they implied was Alaska's best future, Konigsberg reminded his readers. But the oil industry was no partner. It was a dominator of economies and an emasculator of governments. Moreover, the industry had intentionally used its power to insinuate itself into Alaska society, its schools, its entertainment outlets and sports events, confirming and implicitly celebrating Alaskan dependence, and in the long run, subverting public good. Such subversion, Konigsberg averred, is the abnegation of democratic polity, and of government's responsibility to ensure the integrity of the democratic process.

We are not an imperial colony, Konigsberg insisted. But one could be forgiven for mistaking appearances for just such a reality. Little had changed in Alaska's circumstances from the beginning of the century when the salmon industry, the few industrial gold mines, and above all, the Guggenheim Corporation copper mine, railroad, and steamship company prompted James Wickersham to argue in Congress for more federal aid for the territory to combat the power of the great trust. Despite divestiture, the BP-ARCO merger exacerbated Alaska's colonial dependence. The new corporation will have much more control over Alaska jobs as the sole operator of North Slope production. Its investments in technology will control the pace of production. As operator, its leverage on production will be substantial. Moreover, many industry analysts tout natural gas as the future energy source for America; the merger gave BP-ARCO a controlling interest in North Slope natural gas, which some commentators argued was its chief purpose.

Governor Knowles scheduled hearings on the "Charter for Development." In his own statement, the governor insisted that "Alaska cannot—and will not—be beholden to a board of directors in London." But it was a fair question to ask if such dependence could be avoided. At the hearings many Alaskans wanted to make statements. Most favored the charter. Their testimony focused primarily on the question of monopoly. There were critics, and one supporter thought the governor's statement went too far in appeasing them. Corporations would locate elsewhere rather than "fight the resistance of Alaska's leaders," he said. In the BP-ARCO merger hearings, some witnesses raised the issue of the environment, but mostly to agree with industry assertions that development and environmental integrity could be compatible. This was and still is the mantra of pro-development advocacy in Alaska. In an ongoing crusade to open ANWR for exploratory drilling, Senator Murkowski repeatedly insisted that the footprint, the developed area from which drilling and production would be undertaken, could be kept much smaller than in earlier, less technologically advanced endeavors. Besides, the Senator proclaimed, it's barren land. "If they see it for what it is," he said, referring to his Senate colleagues, "they might be convinced that oil can be drilled there using modern technology without doing environmental harm." Environmentalists disagreed; they have called the Arctic coastal plain "America's Serengeti" because of its "wealth of grizzlies, musk oxen, caribou and migratory birds." The coastal plain may appear barren in the middle of a January storm, a frozen waste where for six weeks the sun never rises above the horizon and the wind whips the snow into standing sheets that race each other across miles of dark white tufted hillocks. But only the least sensitive would fail to appreciate the life lying dormant and the haunting beauty of the vastness of nature locked in place, gathering itself for a new burst of life with the return of the sun and the spring thaw. Those supporting development, including the Inupiaq of the North Slope Borough, believe, with Senator Murkowski, that life in the Refuge can be adequately protected. Those who support permanent and exclusive protection for the Refuge believe the line at the frontier edge of development must be drawn along the Refuge boundary. The Gwitchin Athabaskans of Venetie and Arctic Village believe further development of the plain represents an unacceptable level of risk to the caribou upon which they depend for food, and for cultural identity. Is compatibility possible in such circumstances? The oppositional mode of thinking seems to preclude it.

Across Alaska throughout the twentieth century, Native residents, pioneering settlers, and sojourners have looked at the landscape and marveled at its power. But when presented with opportunities for economic advance, they have usually elected to compromise or even sacrifice wilderness values. This phenomenon was not unique to Alaska, or a new experience in America. In 1907 President Theodore Roosevelt wrote to John Muir to explain why he supported the damming of Hetch Hetchy valley in Yosemite National Park. The dam would provide water for the rapidly expanding city of San Francisco. He doubted, Roosevelt told Muir, that "the great majority would take the side of wilderness in a showdown with the material needs of an expanding civilization." Alaskans through the century would have understood Roosevelt and misinterpreted Muir, as well as Robert Marshall, who wanted all of Alaska north of the Arctic Circle set aside as a wilderness preserve. Where Muir and Marshall saw wilderness as the facilitator of human happiness, their opponents saw it as an impediment. Alaskans have seen wilderness as infinite, and therefore have been unconcerned that one swath of development here will make any difference in the preservation of wilderness there. Thus, at the end of the twentieth century, few worried that large-scale tourism companies selling packaged tours represented a pressure that might change the character of Denali Park, or that a railroad connection from the Bering Sea to Canada, urged by Senator Murkowski, would traverse a number of conservation units set aside for their pristine nature. Few have worried that the thousands of visitors to Brooks Camp in Katmai National Park may adversely affect the brown bear population there, or Native cultural resources. Few have considered that increasing sports hunting pressure on sheep in Wrangell-St. Elias National Park and Preserve may be curtailing Native subsistence use of that and other resources, or that commercial fishing in Glacier Bay National Park and Preserve might change the character of that natural marvel. For most Alaskans, economic uses are justified under most circumstances.

In his essay on the concept of wilderness titled "The Wilderness Idea Revisited: The Sustainable Development Alternative," environmental ethicist J. Baird Callicott called for "sustainable development" of wilderness, by which he meant "initiation of human economic activity that does not compromise ecological integrity seriously; and, ideally, economic activity that positively enhances ecosystem health." He gave as an example "extractive reserves" in the Amazon rain forest. There, in some areas, Indians harvest drippings from rubber trees, and cultivate small cleared areas for truck farming, and are protected from loggers, cattle ranchers, miners, and hydroelectric engineers by government laws and regulations. It hasn't worked perfectly, but legislation sensitive to Native survival and to the health of the forest has provided a legal umbrella for compatible uses of wilderness.

ANILCA may represent such an opportunity in Alaska. A judicious reading of that act, cognizant of the threat to wilderness represented by technology-driven, unrestrained economic development, which is the reading the Park Service has been attempting, may represent compatibility for Alaska. In a report written by the Alaska chapter of the National Parks and Conservation Association, *National Parks of Alaska: Conflict, Controversy, and Congress,* the authors relate a promising development in Gates of the Arctic National Park. Soon after ANILCA was passed, tensions developed between the residents of a Nunamuit village within the park boundary and park managers over the use of all-terrain-vehicles for subsistence hunting. Park staff worried that locals were damaging wilderness lands, while locals felt cut off from traditional hunting grounds. Twelve years of negotiation produced a satisfactory agreement. The regional corporation and the Park Service arranged a land exchange, and the Park Service helped facilitate regular access to traditional hunting and gathering sites. Communication, Park Service personnel aver, led to a win-win for all sides. In other Alaska parks, joint federal/state management boards have worked out allocated use of the land for traditional subsistence activity through discussion and debate.

Canadian environmental historian John Sandlos has reminded us that Euro-Americans have always imposed imagined views on the North. They did not see what was actually there. Instead, they clothed the North with fanciful conceptualizations that became the basis for policy. These were several: the North as wilderness; the North as resource factory; the elemental North. The North became the essential ingredient in Canadian identity, the non-British, non-French, non-American element—"the great North and its living whiteness, its loneliness and replenishment, its resignation and release, its call and answer"—that unified emerging Canadian culture. Its main role was as a clean, morally pure, demanding slate on which Canadians could write their values and self-concept. As Douglas West has commented, Canadians "Nordicized" the North, "made it a categorical reflection of themselves and their creative desires." Sandlos points out that in all this Canadian imagining of the North, there was no place for the Native peoples; they were absent. Thus, they were ignored, moved out of the way, marginalized.

As I have suggested, the Americans did much the same in Alaska. They imposed a their own view on Alaska, though a different one than the Canadians'. The American concept of the North was not very Nordic, though there were glimpses of such an idea in Robert Service's rhymes and Jack London's tales. Instead, the American view of the North was western; it was frontier. Far more settlers went to Alaska than went to the Canadian North, a phenomenon still true today. Their goal was, and to a large degree remains, to develop the wilderness, to conquer it and make it over into civilization, into modern American culture. They did not see nature for itself, a living organism where trees exist as trees and streams as streams. Trees were to convert into house lumber and streams were holders of sport fish, as the seas were holders of commercial fish.

Alaskans did share two aspects of the Canadian view. First, they saw Alaska as a resource factory, but one far more were willing to live in, provided that living there included altering the landscape, forcing it into sawmills, salmon cans, copper coils and gold coins and brooches, and today, barrels of oil. Second, they did not see the Natives as who they were. Applying the same policies that had obtained in the American West after the Civil War, their notion was to "civilize" them. As we have seen, capable Native leaders accepted this idea, and made it their own, although the farther any particular group of Natives was physically separated from non-Native settlement, the slower the process of acculturation.

ANCSA and ANILCA changed Alaska, dramatically and permanently, even as many Alaskans missed the significance of the both civil rights and the environmental revolution. ANCSA forced Alaskans to take Alaska Natives seriously, and on their own terms. Those terms were much changed from the images of Natives most Americans held, reflected in Edward Curtis's turn-of-the-twentieth-century photographs: tragic children living meagerly off the resources of the land. Modern Alaska Natives demanded the right to be subsistence harvesters or corporate directors, as their circumstances and inclinations might dictate. That they learned to be as materialist as whites in the dominant culture, and that they claimed the right to be so, should have surprised no one.

Nor should Alaskans have been surprised that, as the national environmental conscience evolved, Americans should single out Alaska as the premier landscape on which to impose their vision of wilderness, imagining the non-urban parts of Alaska to be places where, "in contrast with those areas where man and his works dominate the landscape," "the earth and its community of life are untrammeled by man, where man himself is a visitor who does not remain." Like the Canadian view of the North, this view of wilderness leaves out the Native people. Half of America's designated wilderness is in Alaska. But there are 211 Native villages in Alaska, many of them in or near wilderness areas or conservation units. As suggested above, ANILCA may have created a new kind of American wilderness, one in which human presence is seen as legitimate, provided that our activity is consistent with wilderness values, the protection and preservation of natural systems. But Natives worry that their access to both subsistence resources and economic opportunities may be curtailed by mining and logging companies, on the one hand, and by exclusionist preservationists, on the other. Discussion by all these groups has led to a temporary *modus operandi* that protects ancient needs and interests. For it to become permanent, many agreements will need to be crafted by all of the parties involved. Because of the resilience and new political and economic power of Alaska Native groups, such agreements seem possible.

In the meantime, most Alaskans proceed unaware of conversations between land managers and Natives, or among those who think about environmental values. The view of most Alaskans is occluded by oil prices, and their impact on the expansion or contraction of the Alaska economy. They are also worried about the effect of oil prices on the size of the Permanent Fund dividend. For the vision of most Alaskans has not lifted to the wilderness; it is rooted still in the frontier, and focused on the money.

 ❧ ❧

A recent study commissioned by the Alaska Conservation Foundation found that 84,000 jobs in Alaska for a total income of $2.6 billion, 26 percent of total employment, rely on a healthy environment. The industries counted in the study included commercial fishing, tourism, guiding, sport fishing, wildlife viewing, subsistence harvesting, and government jobs managing natural resources. Jobs tied directly to these industries numbered 55,000, with another 29,000 paid for by the paychecks from direct employment. The oil industry directly generates an estimated 8,870 jobs, and another 24,703 paid for by the paychecks from direct employment, for a total of 33,573. There is considerable crossover in these statistics. Many Alaskans pay for hunting and fishing gear and guides with money earned working directly or indirectly for the oil industry. The money to pay state bureaucrats comes from taxation on oil production. But the study does call attention to the economic value of the environment in Alaska.

Tourism continues to grow. About one-half the 1.4 million visitors to the state in 2000 came on cruise ships. Alaska is now the third most popular cruise destination in the world, behind the Caribbean and the Mediterranean. This mostly passive use of the Alaska environment contributed $282 million to the southeast economy alone in 2000. Ecotourism, including back-country hiking and camping, kayaking, photography expeditions, and the like, has grown exponentially. Denali National Park is the most popular national park in Alaska and attracts increasing numbers of passive tourists who ride busses along the park's single road and ecotourists who trek its wilderness areas. But few Alaskans yet appreciate the economic value of Alaska's environment, and fewer still would be willing to trade the environmental economy for the oil economy. Depending on who sponsors the data, between 72 and 55 percent of Alaskans favored opening the Arctic National Wildlife Refuge to oil drilling in 2000.

It is a tenet of history as a way of thinking and as an academic discipline that understanding the past inevitably changes the future. Collective memory generates community identity, and helps develop purpose. Purpose, a sense of mission or destiny, may engender empowerment, and through empowerment, the capability to shape the future.

Alaska is a young society, and its residents share little collective memory. Congress granted statehood to the territory less than five decades ago. The state's transiency rate is still high; many residents do not intend to live out their careers in the state, retire there, and be buried in the cold, cold ground. And the accessible history of the region, told mostly in romantic videos marketed to the tourist industry, is chiefly a collection of mythic stories about the heroism of sourdoughs, dog mushers, and bush pilots. Only as the collective memory becomes more complete, more comprehensive, and more realistic will it be capable of generating a regional identity, one sensitive to the history and nature of the place, an appreciation of what is there and has been there rather than focused on what isn't yet there. Perhaps commentaries such as this will help hasten that eventuality.

Bibliographical Note

✠ ✠

For this study I have drawn on thirty years of research in Alaska records, including record groups in the Alaska Region of the National Archives and in the Alaska State Archive. The Records of the Office of the Governor of Alaska are a rich mine of material. I have also spent countless hours with film of the Curry-Weissbrodt papers, and with records of the Office of the Secretary of the Interior in the headquarters branch of the National Archives in Washington, D.C. Also important were the Papers of William Lewis Paul in the Manuscripts Division of the University of Washington Library, and the diaries of James Wickersham in the Rasmuson Library at the University of Alaska Fairbanks.

The two most important secondary sources for this study were Peter A. Coates, *The Trans-Alaska Pipeline Controversy: Technology, Conservation and the Frontier* (Bethlehem, 1991), and Donald Craig Mitchell, *Sold American: The Story of American Natives and Their Land, 1867-1959* (Hanover, 1997). Both are essential for an understanding of Natives and environment in modern Alaska. They are probably the best historical studies of Alaska yet developed. Gerald A. McBeath and Thomas A. Morehouse, *Alaska Politics and Government* (Lincoln, 1994), is a very useful reference for understanding contemporary Alaska.

I corroborated my own work with that of other scholars of Alaska, also, including particularly the following. Ted C. Hinckley's books and articles on the period between the Alaska purchase and the Klondike gold rush are essential for understanding that period, particularly his *Americanization of Alaska, 1867-1897* (Palo Alto, 1972), and *Alaskan John G. Brady: Missionary, Businessman, Judge and Governor, 1878-1918* (Columbus, 1982). Morgan Sherwood's environmental history of pre-World War II Alaska, *Big Game in Alaska: A History of Wildlife and People* (New Haven, 1981), is an important study of the early disdain of conservation by Alaska's non-Natives. John Bockstoce's *Whales, Ice and Men: The History of Whaling in the Western Arctic* (Seattle, 1986) is the definitive study.

Ken Coates' formative essay, "The Discovery of the North: Towards a Conceptual Framework for the Study of Northern/Remote Regions," in *Northern Review* (1993-94) is an invitation to scholars of the north to broaden the conceptual context of their work. John Sandlos, in "From the Outside Looking In: Aesthetics, Politics and Wildlife Conservation in the Canadian North," in *Environmental History* (2001) is a significant addition to northern historiography.

Kenneth Philp's article, "The New Deal and Alaska Natives, 1936–1945" (*Pacific Historical Review*, 1981), provides important insight into the evolution of Indian policy in Alaska. Important, also, is Terrence Cole's "Jim Crow in Alaska: The Passage of the Alaska Equal Rights Act of 1945" (*Western Historical Quarterly*, 1992). I noted the relationship between statehood, economic development and Native land rights in "Economic Development and Indian Land Rights in Modern Alaska: The 1947 Tongass Timber Act (*Western Historical Quarterly*, 1990).

For the relationship between Alaska Native claims and oil development, Mary Clay Berry, *The Alaska Pipeline: The Politics of Oil and Native Land Claims* (Bloomington, 1975) and John Strohmeyer, *Extreme Conditions: Big Oil and the Transformation of Alaska* (New York, 1993), are very useful. Also important is Lael Morgan's *Art and Eskimo Power: The Life and Times of Alaskan Howard Rock* (Fairbanks, 1988). Kathie Durbin's *Tongass: Pulp Politics and the Fight for the Alaska Rain Forest* (Corvallis, 1999) examines the development of environmental policy.

Index